MY GODFORSAKEN LIFE

BARBARA SMOKER

MY GODFORSAKEN LIFE

Memoir of a Maverick

THORNWICK

Published by Thornwick 2018
Copyright Barbara Smoker 2018

First published in Great Britain by Thornwick in 2018
Address details for Thornwick can be found at
www.thornwickpress.com
and contact at admin@thornwickpress.com
Thornwick Ltd Reg. No 11063757

A CIP catalogue record for this book is available from the
British Library
ISBN 978-1-912664-02-3

Typeset in 9/14pt Baskerville 10 Pro by Matthew Young
Printed and bound in Great Britain by Clays Ltd, Elcograf S.p.A.

CONTENTS

CHAPTER ONE
IN THE BEGINNING

SAID to be the first ever autobiography, Augustine's *Confessions* charts the course of his life's mental sea-change from freethought to Christianity. My own life-story heads in the opposite direction.

I was just one week old when I was baptised (in June 1923) within the Roman Catholic fold, and the Church's statistical claims of membership always assumed that this ceremony conferred the faith on me for life. ('Once a Catholic, always a Catholic.') Even when, 48 years later, I was elected president of the National Secular Society (NSS), I was generally described in the media – and invariably in the Catholic papers – as a 'lapsed Catholic', however vehemently I insisted that, far from lazily 'lapsing' my Church membership, I had positively repudiated it.

Ironically, my presidency of the NSS for 25 years was not my first presidency, but actually my second, since I was appointed by the headmistress of my secondary convent school to be president of its Legion of Mary *praesidium* from 1937 to 1939. I was known by my school-fellows as 'the saint' – though I must say they never held it against me. Even the headmistress – a nun, of course – told me that I should spend less time in church and more on my homework! Written homework, by the way, was always headed 'JMJ' – for Jesus, Mary, Joseph.

How did I come to be so very Catholic? By inheritance. My father was a devout cradle Catholic; my mother, prior to marrying him, became an equally devout Catholic convert. In middle age they both became Franciscan tertiaries – i.e. lay members of the Franciscan religious order.

SIBLINGS

I must have been three when Mummy asked me and my two-year-old sister Celia if we would like to have a baby in the family, and we both said we would. Asked if we would prefer a baby sister or a baby brother, we opted for a brother. Years later I realised that Dad was also keen on having a son. So Mum said we should pray to Jesus every night at bedtime to send us a baby brother. And we never missed.

Sometime later I was sent to stay with an aunt. One morning she received a letter from the postman, and I remember her standing by the breakfast-table reading it. She said to me 'You've got a new baby sister!' 'No I haven't,' I retorted. 'Yes,' she insisted – 'this letter says so.' 'If I've got anything, it's a baby brother', I protested. I could not believe that Jesus had got it wrong, either deliberately or by mistake; but so it transpired. Because neither Celia nor I could pronounce 'Elizabeth', the baby was saddled with Betty, which in later life she changed to Liz.

During the next thirteen years, there were three more additions to the family – Paula, John and Janet. At least another five babies (including boys) were either stillborn or, being born prematurely – before the days of available incubators – died within a couple of weeks of birth. Dad, whose baptismal name was Gilbert (Gil) hurriedly baptised them, for admission to Heaven – though by that time the horror of hellfire for the unbaptised infant had been replaced by the Augustinian invention of painless Limbo.

In his book *God is not Great*, Christopher Hitchens describes Limbo as a 'mad and cruel idea'. I disagree. Mad, maybe, but not cruel. Christian doctrine had always insisted that salvation depended on baptism, and the manifest unfairness of this doctrine in the case of those who had never received the Christian message led to the mollification of 'implicit baptism of desire' for those who, though ignorant, lived good lives, desirous of doing whatever was right. However, this obviously could not apply to young children, and, since there were only two abodes for eternity in the supposed after-life (Heaven and Hell), it was assumed that unbaptised babies went to Hell – until the theologians annexed a neutral place for them where they would not suffer (though they would never know the bliss of eternally worshipping the deity).

While bereaved parents were thus relieved of the horror of imagining their babies in Hell, they still rushed to have the new-born (and even the still-born) baptised, to gain them a place in Heaven. I actually remember overhearing my mother say outside church to another Catholic woman, who had commiserated with her on the loss of the latest baby, 'Well, the main thing is he was baptised.'

In 2007 Catholic theologians did away with Limbo, and presumably smuggled unbaptised babies somehow into Heaven. (So much for the tenet that the Catholic faith is immutable.)

When, one month before the outbreak of war in 1939, the birth of the youngest child, Janet, was happening, I ran like an Olympic racer to fetch the midwife. (We had no telephone.) She put me in a panic by drawling 'I'll just have my lunch first, m' dear!'. Seeing my consternation, she added 'It's never as urgent as all that, m' dear' – and she did in fact arrive in time.

Me (rather overweight) with Mum, 1924

THE 'GREAT WAR'

An early memory of mine has me standing in our big kitchen and suddenly realising for the first time that being a girl and not a boy meant I would grow up to be a woman, not a man. My immediate inner response, with a flood of relief, was 'Aren't I lucky! I won't have to go in the trenches.'

How I knew about trench warfare I cannot say, as Dad never spoke about the horrors he had experienced as a gunner in four major campaigns of the First World War (known throughout my childhood as the Great War). Some five decades later, whenever anything about that war appeared on television, he would bark 'Switch it off! Switch it off!'. Presumably, though, I had overheard other people talking about it in his absence.

Incidentally, the then Anglican Bishop of Exeter (Lord Salisbury's son) had a letter in the *Times* in 1917 proposing that the 1,100 conscientious objectors imprisoned in Dartmoor, except those motivated by religion, be moved to other prisons where they would be more likely to experience the horror of German bombing raids.

Despite having a close German friend in London before the war, Dad volunteered for the Royal Artillery in 1914, and throughout the war suffered the hell of the trenches – except for a few months in a field hospital when temporarily blinded from mustard-gas. (This trauma was also suffered by a certain Adolf Hitler on the other side, the German gas having wafted back to their own lines.)

It continued to affect Dad's lungs for the rest of his life, with frequent bouts of pneumonia. In 1937, on one of these occasions, with double pneumonia and little hope of recovery, he became, with my mother's permission, a guinea-pig for an experimental drug – one of the sulphonamides, which were precursors of modern antibiotics. Amazingly, he lived for another 41 years, cheating pneumonia again and again. He must have held the worldwide record for the number of times he received the 'last rites', and my mother credited that sacrament (as well as the antibiotics) for his repeatedly pulling through. In his early 80s, when, for the final time, the same 'miracle' occurred, he was manifestly delighted to be alive. Why, I wondered, did his firm belief in a blissful after-life not mitigate his obvious reluctance to experience it?

Dad, Royal Artillery, 1915

In the Somme battlefield mud, Dad found a hollow brass crucifix containing a Latin inscription and relics of three named saints. Probably of Bavarian manufacture, it had almost certainly belonged to a German chaplain, for Catholic priests needed such relics to make a table into an altar for saying Mass. Dad carried this crucifix inside his uniform for the rest of the war, and I imagine he credited it with his improbable survival – though it had manifestly failed to protect the original owner. (It is now in the Royal Artillery museum.)

EARLY LIFE

I well remember an incident that must have taken place at 11 am on 11th November 1927, for I had not yet started school. I am standing with Mummy by the open door to the back-garden of our house, listening to the booming commemorative Armistice guns. I had been enjoined not to breathe a word for the statutory two minutes – which seemed an age to me. That widespread ritual must have been far more pertinent then than now, only nine years after the war.

Another clear memory is of my first day at school, in the spring of 1928. The nun in charge of the kindergarten class, Sister Genevieve, asked me if I knew the ABC. Of course I did: in our family, the toddlers would sing the names of the letters, which Mum used to sing as she went from room to room doing the housework. So I refused to answer such a stupid question. 'How old', I thought, 'does she think I am? Two?' After all, I was actually coming up to five.

In fact, I could already read – as Sister Genevieve

obviously discovered before long – and by the age of eight I was employed as an unpaid literacy tutor in the school. However, there were skills in which I was behindhand, and I remember the humiliation of having to get help in tying the bows on my plimsolls, especially when a girl of my age (who could not read!) was deputed to teach me how to tie a bow.

In those days we did not know anybody with electricity in their homes – that was only for the very wealthy. Streets in London apart from the main roads were still lit mainly by gas, and I well remember the municipal lamp-lighter cycling up our road every evening at dusk with a long pole to ignite each lamp.

Grandma Morris with Celia and me, 1928

HOSPITAL

In October 1929, I developed a body rash of small red spots, and the family doctor was called. (This was not done lightly, since a doctor's visit cost money.) He declared I had Scarlet Fever – one of the law's dreaded 'notifiable diseases'. For some unknown reason, the streptococci of scarlet fever declined to virtually extinct mildness in the next twenty years, but at that time its diagnosis was often a death sentence, and the law of the country required any child who was diagnosed with it or had been in contact with it to be removed from their home and taken to a designated isolation fever hospital. The doctor's verdict therefore meant that not only I, with the rash, but also my two younger sisters, though rashless, had to be taken to the South-East London Isolation Fever Hospital. While our parents were instantaneously deprived – by parliamentary decree – of their three children, I must say I quite enjoyed the adventurous ride in the ambulance to Hither Green.

Because she was not a man, my mother, British born and bred, had no legal right to vote in elections until she was in her thirties.

The only visitors allowed to hospitalised infectious children were ministers of religion – except that one parent was also allowed a brief visit once a month, provided he or (more usually) she had obtained a written permit from a Justice of the Peace. The nurses, in their starched uniforms, resented these rare parental visits, saying that they only left the children upset and tearful. Very few of the other children (there were 24 in our ward, in two rows of 12 beds less than one

9

yard apart) ever had any visits: perhaps it was too difficult for their parents to make the application to a JP.

I remained in the hospital for four months, and my sisters for about half that time, so Mum came (dressed in a sterile hospital gown) three times.

I also received a visit there from a Catholic priest, who said that he had 'met' my mother – which I misunderstood as a chance meeting in the street – and that she had asked him to come and see me and tell me that Uncle Bernard (Dad's younger brother) was to be ordained a priest at Christmas.

Our hospital diet was the same every day: jam sandwiches for breakfast; mince with mash and cabbage for midday dinner, followed by stodgy rice-pudding; and for supper a choice (yes, actually a choice!) of mince or rice pudding left over from dinner and served, I remember, in brown tin mugs. We were also given large doses of cod-liver-oil-and-malt twice a day.

DISCIPLINE

Children, however small, who wet the bed were smacked. But to ask for the bed-pan at an inconvenient time (such as just before doctors' rounds or a meal-time) earned a scolding, though it was not easy to know what the time was or to judge the degree of inconvenience.

In the next bed to mine was a little boy, aged four. One day a nurse put both his arms in splints, and said in a loud voice, so we could all hear, that it was because he picked his nose. After that I was really scared to be seen with my fingers anywhere near my nose, lest the same punishment be meted out to me. Now, of course, I realise that I need not have worried; in hospital parlance, nose-picking was obviously a euphemism for masturbation, of which I knew nothing.

To most of the nurses, masturbation was doubtless a biblical sin, which, it was often avowed at the time, could even cause blindness. So the poor little fellow, wrenched from his home and feeling ill, was cruelly chastised for venturing to comfort himself physically.

Celia was in a bed opposite to mine, while Betty, just turned three, was in a bed at the end of the ward, and probably did not realise that hospitalisation was temporary. She kept crying 'My Mummy wants me! My Mummy wants me!', and when she did so during the night it apparently kept some of the other children awake. So one of the nurses took her to see the big sluice which activated the sanitisation system, and told her she would be thrown down it if she made a noise again at night – a similar tactic to that of the Inquisition showing heretics the instruments of torture.

As her eldest sister, I felt I bore some responsibility for her in the hospital, and was upset by her distress, but did not know how to help her, especially as at first I was not allowed out of bed.

SOCIALISATION

Children who were well enough to leave their beds could socialise. This facilitated, of course, the cross-infection of different strains of scarlet fever and other diseases, sometimes with fatal results. Did the politicians who decreed our kidnapping and herding together not foresee this outcome?

The same men (for at that time almost all MPs were male) made a similar decision ten years later to separate children from their parents in the wartime 'evacuation' from London.

During our out-of-bed socialisation periods, we naturally played competitive games, and these were preceded by the cockney incantation of a scary pledge to ensure there was no cheating. Accompanied by licking one's forefinger, wiping it dry, and passing it across one's throat, it ran: 'See me finger's wet, see me finger's dry – cut me froat if I tell you a lie!' It was as effective as the prevailing adult religious oath. I lost some of my milk teeth while in hospital, but the Tooth Fairy was not around, or at least took no notice of me.

One day Betty disappeared from the ward, and I wondered what had become of her. One was never given that sort of information. I suppose it did not occur to any of the staff that a sibling might feel the need to know. Equally, it did not occur to me that I might ask someone about it. Instead I persuaded myself that Betty had been sent home, and that was a great relief to me. In actual fact, however, she had been diagnosed with Chicken Pox, so had been removed to another ward. Other children then went down with the same disease, so our own ward also became a *de facto* chicken-pox ward. But Betty was not brought back. Afterwards, back home, she blinked continuously for a full year.

CHRISTMAS 1929

On Christmas Eve, without any explanation, my bed was moved, with me in it, to the front of the ward, next to the door. Many years later I discovered that this was the procedure for any patient expected to die within a few hours, so that the body could be taken out to the mortuary without passing any of the other beds. I had apparently caught a lethal strain of scarlet fever while in the ward, but all I knew was that I felt ill, and the movement of the bed shook me up.

Christmas day dawned, and I saw lots of presents with my name on the wrappings piled on my bed. While, with difficulty, I was gradually opening them, a Christmas-tree was being erected in the middle of the ward, by the big open fire. (No central heating in those days.)

Then a nurse came to me and said 'We are asking children who have received Christmas presents to give one of them up for a child who has not had any.' I pointed to a large box of dolls-house furniture, having already thought 'What's the use of dolls-house furniture without a dolls-house?' But the nurse, to whom it no doubt represented a high cost rather than a useless gift, said 'Oh, you don't have to give up the whole box – just one little chair!', and I was ashamed to see her take that one useless little chair out of the box for some hapless child; but I did not feel well enough to argue.

Two nurses began decorating the Christmas-tree and hanging presents on it, and they placed the most beautiful glittery fairy-doll at the top.

Christmas dinner comprised mince, mash and cabbage, just as usual, but before the rice-pudding was brought in, a nurse stood in the doorway and announced 'A kind gentleman has brought in a Christmas pudding for children who would rather have Christmas pudding than rice-pudding. Hands up.' Looking around I was amazed to see how few hands were raised. Probably most of the children had never tasted Christmas pudding and were wary of unfamiliar food. But I thought to myself 'I'll have Christmas pudding, if it makes me sick!' and managed to raise my hand. Whether I managed to eat any of the pudding I cannot remember.

THE FAIRY-DOLL

Then something quite wonderful happened. Father Christmas actually found time on this, surely his busiest day of the year, to come to our ward! He went up to the Christmas-tree and began cutting down the gifts, handing them to a nurse who distributed them around the ward. Last of all, he lifted down that lovely fairy-doll, and unbelievably brought it over to my bed and laid it in my arms.

My sister Celia, aged five, was still in the ward, and years later I said to her one day, 'Remember the Christmas we spent in the fever hospital? I was given the fairy-doll off the Christmas-tree.' 'I know, and I know why you got it.' 'What do you mean, why I got it?' 'Well, my bed was near the Christmas-tree and I heard Father Christmas ask the nurse which little girl in the ward was the most ill, and she said you were.' Rather shocked at such professional carelessness, I asked 'Were you worried to hear that your own sister was so ill?' 'Worried?!' she replied. 'What I thought was, how just like Barbara, pretending to be ill on Christmas Day, so as to get the fairy-doll!'

Everything, however, had to be left in the hospital for good, allegedly because of germs. Anyway, on that Christmas

Day, clasping the fairy-doll, I survived – and still survive, almost nine decades later.

One day, when I was sufficiently recovered to leave my bed, wearing a hospital dressing-gown and slippers, I saw a girl of ten brought in – and wondered why she had not been taken to an adult ward! She beckoned me to her bed, and asked if I could read. Then she opened a children's book to reveal a coloured picture of a goblin. Pointing to the caption under it, she commanded, in a conspiratorial tone, 'Read that!'. I could hardly believe my eyes, as this was my first introduction to published pornography. What it said was 'The wee wee man'! Being English, not Scottish, neither of us had ever encountered the word 'wee' except in the 'rude' context.

RELEASE

Before being allowed to leave the hospital, we had to endure specimen swabs being pushed down our throats, to probe for scarlet-fever germs. I hated this choking procedure, but I remember telling myself that I only had to put up with it once more to be allowed home. Then, when it was carried out again, I was cruelly told that, as my throat was still not clear, I could not go home yet. Celia, meanwhile, was discharged.

Eventually, in February, I passed the throat test, and was told my mother was coming to collect me. I had been counting the days of incarceration, and calculated that I had been in the hospital sixteen weeks and three days.

After breakfast I was taken to another ward to be bathed

and have my hair washed, then I was dressed in home clothes handed in by my mother. She had selected for my coming out my best dress – the black velvet with white lace collar – but the nurse who insisted on dressing me put it on back-to-front. I told her it was wrong, but she thought she knew better.

The first thing Mum said to me was 'You've got your dress on back-to-front!', so I told her it was the nurse's fault. But what really upset her was the cockney accent that her daughters had picked up in the hospital. However, I had also picked up something far worse than that: I had left the hospital incubating the virus of Measles.

Within days I passed it on, not only to my two sisters but also to Mum, so that her mother (Grandma Morris) had to come and stay with us to look after the house and the family. Fortunately, measles was not another notifiable disease for hospital isolation – or if it was, we broke the law, for we stayed at home.

On our eventual recovery from measles, Mum and one of her sisters, Aunty Nell, took the three of us away on a convalescent seaside holiday, together with our fun-loving 11-year-old cousin Joan – who was tragically destined to be killed ten years later in the London Blitz. (Just one of 43,000 Londoners killed in that bombing spree.) After the holiday, Celia and I went back to school, from which we had been absent for almost a year.

With Celia on our
First Communion Day,
June 7th 1931

ARSON

Some time later I caused an incendiary instance of a little learning being a dangerous thing. I knew that the Latin prefix *in-* had a negative significance (as in the word 'infirm') but not that it also had an alternative meaning (as in 'include') – so when I saw the word INFLAMMABLE inscribed in gold on the comb that lay on Mum's dressing-table, I assumed it meant Not Flammable, and decided to put that to the test.

Though at that date we had gas-lighting in our downstairs rooms, the rooms upstairs were lit only by portable candles – one of which stood, conveniently alight, on the dressing-table. So I held the comb in the candle flame – and, of course, it flared up. To save my fingers, I sacrificed the polished surface of the dressing-table, by dropping the burning comb upon it. Quarter of a century later, when Mum gave me her antique rosewood bedroom suite, she apologised that the burn on the dressing-table needed expensive restoration – though I am sure she remembered that it was I who had been responsible for the damage (which I have yet to rectify).

Undoubtedly my accident was not the only one caused by the ambiguity of the word 'inflammable'; before long the Latin prefix was universally omitted from such warnings, at least in English.

Once, when I had done something else that was potentially dangerous, my mother said that she could be sent to prison for it. I had never heard of prison before, and asked her what it was. She told me it was where bad people are locked up, and I asked, in horror, 'Like in a zoo?!' I thought captivity must be wretched for animals, but worse still for human beings. Some forty years later I was to chair the inaugural meeting of Radical Alternatives to Prison, which promoted the idea of community service orders.

Even worse than prison, of course, was capital punishment. After the war, whenever I read or heard on the wireless that a certain murderer was to be hanged at 8 o'clock the next morning, I would watch the clock in a state of petrified horror as the minute hand crept to the appointed time. Years later I would campaign for the abolition of capital punishment – sometimes even sharing a platform with a clergyman, though I was an implacable atheist by that time.

LITURGY

I always enjoyed the mysterious church liturgy of my youth – in those days, of course, all in Latin – and particularly the spooky Lenten service of *tenebrae*, which was the most goose-pimply service of the whole year. In the thirties, our parish priest was probably one of the last in London to retain it. Taking place after dark in the three mid-week evenings before Good Friday, it culminated in the church lights being gradually extinguished while the priest chanted some mantra in Latin, at a higher and higher pitch until the last candle went out.

We had a school chapel – a miniature church – in both my convent schools, and there were crucifixes, statues, and holy pictures everywhere. In the secondary school, we had devotions at the close of some days, varying according to the month's dedication. For instance, in May, dedicated to the Virgin Mary, there would be a procession round the grounds to a grotto – a replica of the one in Lourdes. And I made a miniature of it in our back garden at home. Every day, the loud multi-peal Angelus bell rang out through the school at 12 o'clock. Lessons were immediately suspended while everyone stood for the recitation of the Angelus ('The Angel of the Lord declared unto Mary ...') – one person beginning it, and everyone else responding in unison.

In history, we were told that the alleged gunpowder plot against Parliament was an anti-Catholic frame-up – as many historians now admit it probably was. Since the whole national tradition of November 5th, with its fireworks and effigies of Guy Fawkes (collecting pennies before being burnt on a bonfire), was obviously anti-Catholic, we were not allowed to participate. But our parish priest (the one who performed the medieval *tenebrae*) had a bright idea that we could enjoy fireworks on November 1st – to com- memorate All Saints Day – instead of the 5th; so Catholic children would enviably have a fireworks party four days ahead of the Protestants! Nowadays, this would make no difference: though the Guy Fawkes tradition persists, it is now celebrated from mid-October till mid-November with little knowledge of its historical origins, while enabling the fireworks firms and shops to make huge profits (and keeping the fire brigades busy!).

THOU SHALT NOT

The nun who taught us religion – mainly the Catechism – spent several weeks on the Ten Commandments when we were eight or nine, dealing with each commandment extensively. For instance, 'Thou shalt not kill' (the fifth in the Catholic Church, though, as I learned later, Protestants called it the sixth) not only forbade the mortal sin of murder but such associated venial sins as bad temper. But when she came to the sixth commandment (the Protestant seventh), which contained the unfamiliar word 'adultery', she merely wrinkled up her nose and said 'Nasty!'. So we were left to imagine what it meant – and I assumed it was using rude words and telling rude jokes.

Shortly afterwards, when examining my conscience prior to the weekly confession (mandatory from the age of seven), I thought I ought to confess that I had giggled at a bawdy joke, and I decided it would be easiest to tell the priest I had committed adultery. I remember his asking me what exactly I had done, and I suppose he must have been amused, but he did not explain what 'adultery' really meant.

One of the nuns used to sell confectionery at break-time, and apparently found that her sales plummeted during Lent, when most of the children gave up sweets, so she informed us that chocolate bars were not sweets, they were nutritious food. (This Jesuitical commercialisation made Dad laugh.)

At home we had to wait until midday on Holy Saturday before being allowed to unwrap our Easter eggs. And that was probably after six weeks (except for Sundays) of giving up sweets for Lent – this being expected of us, though not compulsory. I remember Celia's ruse one year when she had agreed to give up eating sweets for Lent, and was caught with a sweet in her mouth – whereupon she explained that it was *eating* sweets she had given up, not *sucking* them!

REVELATIONS

Celia and I played competitive games – sometimes letting Betty join in – and Rule Number One in our games was always 'No praying'. We obviously believed in its efficacy – and supernatural favouritism was not the facility being tested.

My poor showing in such skills as ball-games was no doubt exacerbated by extreme short-sightedness, which actually remained undiagnosed until after my ninth birthday. Our convent school, which concentrated on our moral and spiritual health, took little interest in physical wellbeing, and Mum refused to believe that any of us children had any defects – even though, as far as myopia was concerned, she knew that Dad was very short-sighted. However, my mother was persuaded by Aunty Nell to take me in 1932 to the Moorfields Eye Hospital. To facilitate a diagnosis she had to put belladonna drops in my eyes every day for a week to dilate the pupils. Nowadays it takes a few minutes.

Moorfields was a short walk from Dad's office (Smoker & Chapman) in Foster Lane, and on my second visit to the hospital Mum took me afterwards to the office. A new-fangled telephone with a large dial had just been installed there, and adults were crowding round the instrument in amazement. We were told that instead of having to ask the operator to connect you to the required number, you could get it automatically yourself by dialling the number with your forefinger. It was clearly one of the wonders of the world.

The first day that I went out wearing glasses I just stood stock-still in astonishment in front of a tree, on which I could actually see separate leaves instead of the green cloud that I had assumed was what everyone saw.

One of my main interests in those days, as with most young people, was food – especially dinner. Chicken was costly, so was only for Easter Sunday. Beef, rather expensive nowadays, was then good value, and Mum reckoned that having an 'aitch-bone' of beef, which could last our family of five from Sunday to Wednesday, was the most economical way of feeding us like royalty. So we had roast beef with Yorkshire pudding and lots of vegetables on Sunday, cold on Monday, mince on Tuesday and stew on Wednesday. Grandma Morris used to come over from Streatham for the day every Tuesday, and I remember asking her if she really liked mince. 'Not particularly', she replied. So I told her she came on the wrong day of the week.

MISSIONARY ZEAL

Children grew up more slowly in those days than they do now, and I was ten before I worked out that Father Christmas was mere fiction, concocted by adults to make fools of children. That is the way I saw it. Really angry, I confronted my mother: 'You have been telling me lies for years about Father Christmas!' On the defensive, she replied 'Well, not really lies – Father Christmas is a symbol of generosity.' 'But that's not what you said – you said he was an old man who came down the chimney with our Christmas presents.'

Refusing to let her off the hook, I decided to help other children stand up to the Father Christmas deception, and began a self-righteous campaign around the neighbourhood, with the same missionary zeal that impelled me to donate most of my pocket money to the missions taking the true religion to babies in Africa and China. It prefigured the various campaigns of my adult years, and I now regard missionary zeal as an innate trait, irrespective of its manifestations.

I must have been betrayed by one of the Costello children – a large Catholic family, into which my sister Celia was to marry after the war. Their father accosted me with the accusation that I was telling his children there was no Father Christmas. 'It's the truth!' I protested. 'But some of them are younger than you are.' I could not see that that made any difference: I was saving them from being made fools of, as I had been. But there was no arguing with authoritative adults.

Because public libraries at that time denied admittance to children under ten years of age and my first school lacked books, I had never read any of the children's classics. This horrified my secondary-school English mistress, who suggested I begin with *Treasure Island*. I obediently borrowed it from the school library, but to me it was just silly boys' stuff. However, on returning the book to its shelf, I found the same author's *Dr Jekyll and Mr Hyde*, and decided to try that. I literally could not put it down. That melodramatic allegory of good and evil was the most memorable reading experience of my life.

However, I experienced a real personal horror one winter evening shortly after dark. I was on my way home from school alone, on a deserted footpath, when a man suddenly confronted me and reached out his hands to my throat. I screamed at the top of my voice – to such good effect that he ran away, no doubt expecting people to emerge from adjacent houses. As I did. But nobody emerged. I ran home, shaking like a leaf, but told no-one about the incident. Nor did it occur to me that the man ought to be reported to the police. I think now that he could have been no more than a moronic prankster, merely play-acting for a laugh.

Aged 14 to 15, I wrote an entire romantic novel, Victorian both in tone and period, and the kind aunt of one of my school friends typed it out for me; but (fortunately) it was never published.

AWARDS

For Prize-giving we had to wear white gloves, and gloveless girls who were awarded a prize or a coloured sash would desperately borrow a pair.

Every Catholic school in the diocese of Southwark was subject to an annual religious knowledge inspection. Our diocesan inspector, early in 1939, not knowing that Celia and I were sisters, concluded that we both deserved a silver medal – but said he was not allowed to award more than one in the same school. So he turned to the headmistress for advice. She obviously ought to have said that Celia, being the younger, was the true winner, but she perversely named me, on the grounds that it was my last year at school and therefore my last chance for a medal, whereas Celia would have another chance in 1940.

This injustice was compounded on Prize-winning Day, when, as the certified medal-winner, I was awarded the prize of a daily missal – in Latin, of course, but with the English translation alongside. It was a welcome gift, as it covered every day of the year, unlike my existing missal which covered only Sundays and important festivals. However, seeing that Celia was justifiably aggrieved at the unfairness of it, I offered her the missal; but she spurned it.

The unfairness was further compounded by her having to leave school a few months later, when we were 'evacuated' from London – owing to the minor circumstance of the Second World War.

EVOLUTION

Amazingly, until after the war I never came across the word 'dinosaur', which nowadays is in every child's vocabulary from nursery-school age. Though we lived near the Crystal Palace, and used to be taken to the Christmas circus there until the glass structure burnt down in 1936, I had never visited the 19th-century model dinosaurs in the grounds.

The theory of evolution was not on our school syllabus, but I worked it out for myself through going alone on Saturdays to Horniman's Museum, which was within walking distance of our house. The animal skeletons on display there were arranged in evolutionary sequence, and I came to the obvious conclusion.

I was rather worried about its doctrinal implications until we had a new lay biology mistress, who told us that the Church (meaning the Vatican) had just declared that it no longer regarded belief in evolution as heretical – so long as it was seen as God's method of creation, culminating in the emergence of the first human beings, in whom God exclusively implanted immortal souls. I doubt if the other girls paid much heed to this revelation, but it came as a great relief to me.

It was several years before I reasoned that this capitulation by the Church was far from total, for the special creation of a human soul (synonymous with 'mind') meant that human evolution entailed only the body, separate from the soul. And the Catechism definition of the soul as the seat of 'intelligence and will' had long puzzled me, since our pet cat exhibited both – but it did not occur to me to confide in the nuns, or anyone else, about such troubling anomalies.

Percipient evolutionists are more likely to be biologists than philosophers, let alone theologians. In a recent physiological book review about the truly awe-inspiring complexity of the immune system, Henry Marsh makes the following comment. 'It is hard to conceive of a divine intelligence smart enough to design it. It is the product, instead, of many millions of years of trial and error.' Yes indeed! The true creative force of evolution is one of long-term haphazard trial and error.

PORTENTS OF WAR

The evening of the Crystal Palace fire in 1936 is clear in my memory. A visitor told us about it, and then it was on the wireless. Some of my school-friends were allowed to go out to see it, and described being caught up in a huge crowd, but I merely stood in our back-garden mesmerised by the red of the night sky. Four years later, in September 1940, I witnessed the same night-sky phenomenon again.

This time it was caused by the first incendiaries in the London Blitz, mainly on the docks and in the City. On 30 December, trying to reach the City office where I was a clerk, I was to experience unquenched fires in person. Between those dates, a direct hit on Aunty Nell's house in Streatham killed my cousin Joan.

In my father's youth, a family friend (who, but for WW1, would have become his brother-in-law) was a Bavarian, who, on the outbreak of that war, had to return to Germany. The family friendship being renewed between the wars, I spent a month's holiday in 1938 with his family in Bavaria.

While German-schoolboys spent the summer break at a Nazi military camp, their sisters were sent to stay with strangers for a few weeks of domestic service. Our little maid was nine years old. Her surname was Neunteufel (literally nine devils), which amused me.

A young Nazi who spoke good English because he was a football journalist was enlisted to take me around, and I remember his saying, as we passed a synagogue in the process of being demolished, 'Places won't be needed any more for those terrible people'. Years later I asked what became of him, and was told he was killed in the 1940 invasion of Norway. People I have told about him have said 'Served him right!'; but he had been indoctrinated – as I had, in a different regime – and I do not believe in independent freewill.

As a corollary to its implacable doctrine of freewill, the Church teaches (or taught) that children reach the age of reason, and therefore become responsible for their actions, at about seven years. When my brother John was six, and Mum was reprimanding him for some misdemeanour, he remonstrated, knowledgeably but paradoxically, 'You can grumble at the others but not at me, because I have not reached the age of reason yet.' On another, similar, occasion, he raised the perennial theological problem of freewill by asking, again astutely, 'Aren't I the way God made me?'

MUM'S GENEALOGY

My mother's real name was Amy Cecilia Morris, but as there was another Amy Morris in her school she was known by her middle name – and thenceforth was known as Cis, for short.

Her father, William Morris – not the famous William Morris – came from the Welsh Black Mountains, leaving there for London in his orphaned teens to make his fortune. He got a job in a fish-shop in Forest Hill, where a local girl, Barbara Pullen, was no doubt a customer. When he made her pregnant, there was a quick Anglican church wedding (essential in those days). He had to falsify his age, as he was only 19. She was 21.

They had seven children, of whom six survived childhood. Bert, the eldest, also falsified his age – not for marriage but to enlist in the Boer War, from which Grandma had to buy him out. After Bert, came Elsie, Edie and Nell, followed by Fred and my mother, the youngest.

Having been born eight years before the 1870 Education Act, Grandma Morris never went to school, and always regretted it. No better than semi-literate, she was a skilled seamstress and made the upholstery for Samuel Cody's pioneer aeroplane in 1908. She was also adept at plucking chickens and skinning rabbits. She loved her scurrilous Sunday newspaper, which lasted her the whole week – but with rather flawed understanding of the news items. When she had to fill in a form, my mother used to do it for her, leaving her to add her signature. It took her several minutes to dip the pen in the ink-bottle and put pen to paper.

She had two really famous cousins. One was Frank Woolley, the great England cricketer. He gave his celebrated cricket bat to my brother John – who, deciding to take it boastfully to school, unfortunately left it on the bus.

The other renowned cousin was James Henry Pullen, who would now be diagnosed as autistic but was known in those days as an 'idiot savant'. A talented painter and meticulous model maker, especially of ships, he was befriended by the then Prince of Wales (later Edward VII). Many of his artefacts are now on permanent display in the Langdon Down Museum, Teddington.

As for my maternal grandfather, I am almost certain that he was a compulsive gambler – and this could have contributed to the breakup of his marriage. Aunty Edie, in her old age, said to me one day: 'Father used to go to Epsom, and come back without any money.' Another indication is that John and I have both inherited the gambling gene – John betting mainly on football and I mainly on horse-racing. I am sure it is an inherited trait. Though Mum was not really a gambler, she was a shopaholic, and the two traits are probably two sides of the same inherited condition. My youngest sibling, Janet, exhibits a bit of both, though necessarily self-restrained. When she was about ten, she often asked me on Saturdays, after receiving her week's pocket-money, 'Will you put thrupence on Piglet for me?' (At that time, Lester Piggott was a teenage apprentice jockey.)

Another thing that most of us inherited from the Welsh William was his blood group, B, which is rare among the indigenous English but common in the Black Forest. One of his descendants, Martin (Celia's youngest), has the very rare group AB, apparently from the merging of his father's A with his mother's B.

The solitary genesis, however, of the deep red colour of my wavy hair is a mystery. People used to stop me in the street and say 'What beautiful hair you have!' But Mum made it clear that natural looks were undeserved. Even so, when,

Future mother, aged about 14 (school-leaver) and 20 (Dad's fiancée)

many decades later, my hair colour began to give way to old-age white, I really mourned it – and archived the last russet lock.

When Mum was three, her father returned to Wales with a 'lady friend', and either married her there bigamously or simply did not bother about another wedding. It was suggested to us that he cared nothing for his family, but that cannot be true as he actually kidnapped the two youngest so as to take them back to Wales with him. But Fred escaped and revealed his father's whereabouts, so Cis (at that time Amy) was rescued.

She was a lifelong avid reader, and would discuss the characters created by George Eliot or Thomas Hardy as though they were real people she had known.

From the age of seven, Aunty Edie had only one leg. The other was amputated because she was pushed over in her school playground and the leg turned gangrenous. Grandma always kept the handwritten letter she had received from the surgeon. It read: 'Madam, I fear we must remove the leg or the child will surely die.' Owing to her piteous disability, Edie was given a free education in a private school and taken on holiday to China by a retired colonel. Through him she met a young army officer, 'Teddy', the son of an earl.

While Teddy was away fighting in the Boer War, she claimed he had proposed marriage to her, and she apparently believed it herself though it seems unlikely. On his return, he denied the engagement and she sued him for 'breach of promise'. This yielded a small annuity but cost her all her posh friendships.

In her youth Edie had a 'peg-leg', but by middle age it had evolved into a life-like artificial leg. In her early eighties, my parents had her to stay with them for a short holiday in their Sussex retirement home, but then realised that she was too demented to be sent back to her lone council flat in Stockwell – though they were really too old themselves to look after her. To give Mum a break, I went down for a couple of days and slept in Edie's double-bedded room. Going to bed, she removed her artificial leg, and, to make sure she did not put it on again during the night and go wandering, I took it to the further end of the room – only to see her actually hop across to retrieve it!

Meanwhile, my sister Paula, being a nun, managed to get her into a convent care-home, but this cost much more than Edie's state pension and annuity. Dad was having to meet the deficit until Celia, having had years of experience as a councillor in Lewisham, managed to persuade Lambeth Borough Council to admit responsibility, Edie having lived in the borough for all her 83 years. Before telephoning the head of the council's care department, Celia cleverly ascertained the name of the chairman of the relevant committee. Getting nowhere with the department, she said 'Well, if you're unable to help, I must just have a word with Mr (so and so); he is always so helpful'. And the official relented.

Edie was given a furry toy cat, which she loved – stroking it all the time. This inspired my poem 'Felix', which I quote at the end of this book. It follows the true story, except that by poetic licence I changed the Boer War to the Great War, multiplied the original Teddy, and killed him/them.

The poem was read out at my sister Betty's funeral, because, succumbing to Alzheimer's, she had similarly been given a baby-doll, which she cared for as a real baby.

DAD'S GENEALOGY

My paternal grandfather, William (another William) Smoker, was a cobbler who made bespoke shoes and riding-boots for the local gentry. He married a nanny/governess, Julia Barsby, though he was a staunch Unitarian and she an equally staunch Catholic. Not only did he have to agree to their wedding being in a Catholic church but also to promise that all children of the union would be raised as Catholics.

No doubt Grandma spent their four decades of devoted married life trying to convert him, but he was too rational to accept the theology, though his brother Jim's daughters were lay preachers in a Wesleyan chapel. Grandma had the effrontery to baptise her husband, without his consent, on his death-bed – presumably so that they could be reunited in Heaven. I cannot recall how I know this, but I must have heard it, directly on indirectly, from my aunt Isabel, who would undoubtedly have endorsed her mother's high-handed action.

Of Dad's other siblings, there was an older brother, Wilfred, as well as the younger Bernard. His favourite sister was Janet, a proficient linguist, who, having served as a nurse on the Great War's Western Front, then married, had two children, and sadly died in her early 40s of 'consumption'. My youngest sister is named after her. Dad's two unmarried

Bernard (the priest), Agnes, Gilbert (Dad), Isabel and Wilfred

sisters, Isabel and Agnes, were both strictly traditional and always lived together.

How upset they were when, after the Second Vatican Council, the old liturgical Latin was replaced by mid-Atlantic English (admittedly banal). Even worse was the consecrated host being placed in one's hand instead of on the tongue, and this was becoming the practice in one church after another. 'There won't be a church left soon that we can go to!' moaned Isabel – usually the spokesperson for the two. On the Chestertonian view that the reformation was arrant theft, she would declare when passing a grand reformation church, 'Of course, that really belongs to us'.

She was traditional also in secular matters: for instance, when, in old age, she was in a hospital where, in the modern fashion, the patients were addressed by their personal names, she gave her name as 'Miss Smoker'. The response being 'No, your first name', she insisted 'I prefer to be called Miss Smoker'.

She never made any secret of her estimation that my father had married beneath him, and I remember her grudging appraisal of my mother: 'Well, she has certainly been a good mother to you children'.

However, she was tastefully and skilfully creative. She was generous with her beautiful home-made gifts and liked arranging my red hair in ringlets. But while helping one of Wilfred's daughters to dress for her wedding, Isabel told her that the unmarried state was 'the higher state'; and a generation later she summoned the fiancé of one of her great-nieces to a premarital cross-questioning which, he told me, put Wilde's Lady Bracknell to shame.

So at least my paternal family background was God-fearing, law-abiding, and, indeed, exemplary – yet I was presumably programmed in my DNA to evolve as a perpetual rebel against corporate authority.

ECONOMICS

Before volunteering for the army in 1914, my father had worked as a commercial traveller for a firm of Japanese importers, and he fell in love with Cis, the teenage 'lady typewriter' in the office there. They corresponded during the war, and she celibately awaited his happy homecoming after the war in 1919.

Back in Civvy Street, Dad decided to set up his own business, with a partner, for Japanese imports – in those days, mainly silk kimonos, which English ladies wore as

My parents in retirement

dressing-gowns. The firm did well enough for him to marry –
Cis having become a Catholic meanwhile – and the wedding
took place in June 1922. By the time of my mother's death in
1992, they had 36 descendants.

A family anecdote amusingly captures Dad's resourceful-
ness. One Saturday morning Dad took a batch of Japanese
scarves to a London street market, only to find that every stall
was already taken. Seeing that one stall held nothing but a
pile of marrows, probably from the stall-holder's allotment,
Dad bought up his entire stock and took over the stall.

Though the family was by no means wealthy, we were
always well fed, and Dad managed to meet the priority of
Catholic school-fees for us all; Mum remaining a full-time
mother. However, seizure by Japan of the Chinese coastal
region led in 1937 to a British boycott of Japanese goods.

The effect of this on Dad's business was compounded by his being hospitalised at the time with pneumonia. Otherwise, he might have saved the firm by turning to merchandise from other countries, which his business partner had not the confidence to do. By the time he left hospital (thanks to sulphonamide medication), it was too late. In his ultra-strict code of business ethics, the concept of limited-liability companies was immoral, so he had to pay his creditors a hundred per cent – which would clean him out.

I remember the evening he came home and sat at the dinner-table giggling. 'What are you laughing at?' asked Mum. 'Well, I've got no money and no job, so there is nothing else to do but laugh.'

He then contacted his younger brother Bernard, who by now was the senior priest in a large wealthy parish, and asked if he had any parishioners who might give him a job. There was one who was manager of the British branch of his Irish family's construction company, and he took Dad on – still convalescent – to sell a group of newly-built bungalows in Surrey. Dad would lie on the bed in the show-house until he heard someone coming, then he would get up and give them his spiel; with some success. When the firm's chief accountant fell ill, Dad took over the position temporarily, and it turned out to be a permanent promotion. On the outbreak of war in 1939 he advised his employer to switch from bungalows to roads and hospitals. The firm prospered, and became a major company.

It was one of the myriad sticking-plasters to staunch the carnage of World War.

CHAPTER TWO
IN TIME OF WAR

TWO DAYS before the declaration of war on 3 September 1939, London school-children became 'evacuees'. Although I had already left school in July, I joined its exodus into rural Surrey, together with Celia, Betty and Paula. I would otherwise be staying at home on my own, as Dad was working elsewhere and Mum was transported into rural Kent with John and Janet, as a mother with two babies. She gave the four of us strict instructions on departure to stay together, and especially that one of us should look after Paula, who was only seven.

Our school's evacuees gathered at the Forest Hill railway station, each of us shouldering the container of a gas-mask, issued the previous year. I overheard Reigate mentioned as a possible destination, so when Dad surprisingly turned up at the station I was able to give him that news. I stupidly assumed that he had somehow just happened to be in the neighbourhood. Later, I realised he must have felt impelled to keep track of his children while governments were threatening to legalise resumption of the satanic massacre that had devastated his early twenties.

We were detrained at Merstham, in Surrey, a village

designated a 'safe' area, where every resident with a spare room had evacuees thrust upon them. No-one could accommodate four together, but we were kept as close as possible, Celia and Paula being dumped on a most resentful newly married couple and Betty and I on the next-door older couple, who were very much kinder. For a week or two some of our own school-teachers remained in the village with us, but they gradually decamped, as did many of the children.

On the first Sunday morning, a group of us were taken to Redhill, to the nearest Catholic church for Mass. At the same time, Neville Chamberlain was delivering his historic announcement that the country was at war. Leaving the church, we were ambling along the pavement when suddenly the air-raid siren sounded. It's rise and fall – dubbed Moaning Minnie – turned one's stomach. Everyone started running, but with no idea where to. We ended up in a shop, and a few minutes later the steady wail of the All Clear siren pierced the air. It had not been a genuine air-raid at all – merely the erroneous identification of a plane. The panic, however, was genuine.

Mum, unable to tolerate the family being split up, prevailed upon Dad to find a house to rent in a 'neutral' area, and he found one in Uncle Bernard's extended suburban Surrey parish, where we were all soon reunited. But war is unpredictable; the house we moved into proved more vulnerable than the London house we had left.

Though I had always been horrified by the idea of warfare, I have to admit that, when war was declared, and for some years afterwards, I was convinced that, unlike the First

World War, the Second was justified, in order to defeat the German Nazi regime.

I now realise that without any external armed interference, populations living under a dictatorship will generally succeed, however belatedly, in overthrowing it. Hitler was lucky enough to survive several assassination attempts by his own people, but even without the Allied victory his luck would not have held indefinitely; there would have been German regime change, war or no war. And war invariably does more harm than good.

Though it had been ostensibly on behalf of Poland that Chamberlain declared war in 1939, the outcome, as far as that country was concerned, was negative. The eventual Allied victory merely swapped Soviet for Nazi domination. Not until fifty years later did Poland herself (embroiled with her own Catholic Mariolatry and inspired by the first Polish pope) spearhead the overthrow of imperialist Soviet communism – without a war.

Even the six-million Jews, with others, who died in the Nazi death camps were themselves war victims – for only in the isolation of war could gas-chambers be built. When the pope (Pius XII) was told about them, he turned a blind eye to this criminal invention. So, shamefully, did the Red Cross – so as to preserve its mandatory wartime neutrality.

As for the saturation bombing (both British and German) of civilian cities – for which Churchill was as culpable as Hitler – it was totally unjustified, and failed to elicit a demand for surrender.

I would not, however, describe myself even now as a

pacifist, since I would support genuine self-defence, rather than turning the other cheek.

THE BLITZ

By the end of 1939 I volunteered as a spare-time recruit in the Youth Auxiliary Service Corps, set up by the Home Secretary, James Chuter Ede. I was deployed around the neighbourhood to help people erect a Morrison shelter in their living-rooms – except that they were usually better at assembling it than I was. But I did score 100% for theoretical poison-gas recognition.

Meanwhile, I had to enlist in the world of employment. This, in our particular class culture, meant an office job in central London. Tertiary education was of course, only for boys.

I therefore set off one morning for an employment bureau in the City, Dad having told me that, as a privately educated and lady-like school-leaver, I should ask for a salary of 25 shillings (£1.25) a week. I accordingly entered that sum on the form I was given to fill in by the woman in charge of the bureau. When I handed it back to her, she exclaimed 'Twenty-five shillings, and no experience!'. But I refused to budge. She then sorted out half-a-dozen cards giving the names and addresses of firms with vacancies for young women like me, and, handing me the batch, pointed out that one of them, a life-insurance company, was actually offering 25/-, the rest only £1. She suggested I went to the high payer first, though she thought there was little chance of their taking me on. So there I went, and was glad to be able to go back to her to say I had been given the job.

The system was that half of the first week's earnings and half of the second had to be paid to the bureau, and the standard working week was five days of eight hours each and four hours on Saturdays, plus unpaid overtime. So for the first two weeks I earned threepence (one-and-a-quarter new pence) and thereafter six pence (two-and-a-half pence) per hour.

I worked in that office for almost three years, with a long return journey by train and bus. This became hazardous with the start of the Blitz – which also added to our workload, insurance money being paid out on the war dead. One evening, faced with hopeless queues for buses, I ran the last three or four miles home, and for weeks I used to approach our house praying that it was still standing and all the family were safe.

On one occasion I had just arrived home when an air-raid warden came to say we had to leave the house immediately as there was an unexploded bomb behind it. I protested that I was just about to have my dinner, but was not allowed to stay to eat it. We were taken to a community hall for the night, and Uncle Bernard turned up there, saying he could accommodate one member of the family in the presbytery. Mum decided that it should be me, as I was the one who had had no dinner.

I was given a meal, then the spare bedroom, and Uncle said that if there was an air-raid during the night he would get up and I could, if frightened, join him. There was indeed a very noisy raid, so I went to find him, but only located the housekeeper and young maid, in their dressing-gowns, in the kitchen. They laughed at the idea that an air-raid would wake Father Smoker up, so I stayed with them till the 'All Clear' siren sounded.

During another air-raid, the whole family, apart from Janet who had been put up to bed, was huddled in our hall-way (supposedly the safest part of a house), when there was a loud explosion. Mum flew up the stairs to Janet, and found her, awake and wide-eyed, sitting up in her cot, covered with plaster from the ceiling but uninjured. After that, our sitting-room windows were boarded up for the room to be used as a sheltered bedroom for nine of us, including Grandma Morris. (I had to sleep in an armchair.)

Early on 30 December 1940, at the height of the London Blitz, I attended Mass in a City church and then conscien-tiously spent the rest of the morning trying to get into work – stepping over prone firemen asleep on the pavements with their empty hoses, and keeping a wary eye cocked for the flaring fragments dropping from the roof-tops. But the police had cordoned off our office, since an incendiary bomb in its courtyard had left a fire burning. So eventually I went into a park to eat my luncheon sandwiches before boarding a bus to Waterloo for the train home.

A few months later, the Blitz having come to an end, the family moved back to south-east London – to a good sized house in Catford Hill, with a tributary of the river Ravens-bourne, a rowing-boat and landing-stage at the bottom of the garden. Dad acquired an allotment ('Dig for Victory') a short distance up-stream, and used to row there with his gardening tools and bring vegetables back in the boat.

Approaching the age of 19, when war-service conscription would probably have condemned me – like several of my school-friends – to work in a munitions factory, I escaped that horror by volunteering for the Women's Royal Naval Service. But I was never one of those who vilified conscientious objectors as cowards – on the contrary, I remember saying, wearing my WRNS uniform, that they were really the brave ones.

IN UNIFORM

I was told to learn the Morse code before reporting for duty as a 'Wren' at HMS Cabbala. This was a land-locked training 'ship' in Lancashire – where a three-year course compressed into six months was to turn me into a wireless telegraphist. I also had to get used to the iconic stiff collar, with studs and tie, like the uniform of civilian businessmen and lawyers.

The camp held a thousand trainees, male and female, and at Christmas 1942 I was horrified to find that no arrangement had been made to provide 'liberty boats' for the Catholics to attend Mass on Holidays of Obligation – of which at that time the Church stipulated two in early January (the 1st and the 8th). I therefore requested an interview with the most senior WRNS officer, to inform her that attending Mass on those days was a religious obligation for Catholics. The imaginary liberty boats were therefore provided before dawn (in the snow), to enable me and other Catholics to leave the camp in time to reach the local Catholic church for the first Mass on each of those days. (How my co-religionists must have blessed me for the privilege!)

On 'passing out' as a wireless telegraphist, I served for six months on a Fleet-Air-Arm station. Though it was merely engaged in training aircraft crews, it often managed to lose one of the planes, complete with crew – the plane, of course, being the more important loss.

Then I volunteered for overseas service. As I was below the age (21) to be sent abroad without parental permission (though that obviously only applied to girls, not boys), I had to ask both my parents for permission. They each said I must ask the other, so I told them separately that the other had given me the required permission. That devious tactic worked, and they both signed the form.

I was then quartered in a crowded central London building, requisitioned as a corral for wrens awaiting transport to some overseas theatre of war. That could mean anywhere in the British Empire – at that time covering a third of the habitable globe, mostly tropical.

Subjected to squad drill in an adjacent residential square, my shabby number-one uniform was condemned by an inspecting WRNS officer, who insisted I buy a new suit. (Unlike women in the Army and Air-force, we had to buy our own uniforms.) I compromised by buying a new skirt only. This was wasteful enough, as I never wore it – bell-bottoms being worn in transit and, for the remainder of my naval service, white tropical uniforms being *de rigueur*. That prodigal WRNS officer has always been on my hate-list.

In WRNS uniform prior to demobilisation,
November 1945

Another wasteful item was the beautiful posh leather-rimmed sun-helmet issued to each of us – though at least we were not expected to pay for that. Though cumbersome, it had to be carried from posting to posting and home again, but was never authorised as part of the uniform of the day. I had no opportunity, therefore, to wear mine, much as I loved it, and on my return to civilian life I handed it in as instructed. (I wished later that I had lied, saying it had been stolen – as in fact many of my other possessions had been.)

The remainder of my wartime experience was served mostly with the Eastern Fleet in Trincomalee, Ceylon (now

Sri Lanka). Following a hazardous sea voyage through the Mediterranean (described below), I personally saw no enemy action during my so-called active service – though it held its own perils. Not least, there were the tropical diseases. For one of them, amoebic dysentery, I was actually prescribed ten injections of arsenic (to kill the amoeba, if not me) – nowadays superseded by a simple pill.

ON THE HOME FRONT

Throughout my overseas service I was naturally worried about the peril faced (and suffered) by my family back home.

Betty was injured by a 'doodle-bug' – the German V1 rocket – which fell one evening on a social club in Forest Hill, whence she had gone with her boyfriend. When she failed to return home, Dad made enquiries and learnt about the rocket incident, whereupon he spent the rest of the night contacting all the local hospitals to trace her. On his second call to one of them, he was told she had been admitted there, with mainly flying-glass injuries. For convalescence she went up to our paternal grandmother's in Southport, the town where, coincidentally, she was to die seven decades later – after marriage, three children, two grandchildren, one great-grandchild, and ten years of appalling Alzheimer's.

My three youngest siblings were also involved in a rocket incident – this time the later V2 rocket, which, unlike the V1, made no warning noise. It fell on Greenwich Park on a lovely sunny afternoon. It was presumably a Wednesday, as it was John's half-holiday from his Catholic secondary school, St. Joseph's College, Beulah Hill. He made his way

Betty, 1946

to Greenwich to meet the two girls from the Ursuline Convent there, and, against the parental instruction always to go home directly from school, the three of them went into the park.

Looking up to the sky, Paula saw the V2 come to the end of its journey, right above them. Shouting 'Lie down!', she pushed Janet to the ground and lay on top of her, John being seated on a low wall beside them. The ensuing explosion was very close, with many people injured and probably killed. Paula hurriedly took the other two home – telling them on the homeward bus to say nothing about their experience, as she thought she would be in trouble for it. They both obeyed her, and this repression no doubt exacerbated the nightmares which they all three suffered for years afterwards.

AT SEA

Bound supposedly for South Africa, we were taken north(!) to Gourock (Firth of Clyde) for the first leg of our journey. There we boarded a peacetime luxury liner, SS Arundel Castle, that, furnished with 15-inch guns, had been commandeered as a troopship, designated an armed merchant cruiser. It was hardly a luxury cruise, however, with nine of us bedded in a cabin designed for two – not to mention the threat of the Luftwaffe in south-eastern occupied France, awaiting our large assembled convoy as it sailed past Algiers. They bombarded us twice.

The first raid did little damage to the convoy, and the convoy's guns destroyed eight German bombers. Looking through a porthole at a patch of sea and sky, I saw a man jump out of a burning plane, open his parachute and drop into the sea. My patriotism giving way to humanitarianism, I turned to a naval lieutenant standing behind me and asked whether we would be picking him up. 'We wouldn't stop for our own', he replied, 'let alone for them.'

This was not entirely true, however. In the second raid, the following day, one of our ships was sunk by a German bomb, and, though the convoy did not slow down, a naval destroyer did stay behind to pick up survivors.

Next day, there was an announcement on our ship's tannoy system as follows. 'If you are writing letters home and want to mention yesterday's incident, you may not say more than the BBC Home Service news item about it, as in this recording: "One of our convoys was attacked in the Mediterranean yesterday; damage was negligible".'

After queueing to go through the Suez Canal, the convoy sailed along this narrow passage, and I was captivated by the close-up view of the Egyptian bank, especially the camels.

Then we sailed down the Red Sea to Aden. Waiting there for several days, we were given shore-leave. This gave me the opportunity to find a Catholic church, alone, for Confession and Sunday Mass. I was then picked up by a flirtatious resident Englishman. In a taxi with open ventilation, which produced a welcome cool breeze, he took me to all the touristy places. He then bought me a new dress – for which he played double-or-quits with the shopkeeper. (And had to pay double.)

The next stop for our convoy was Mombasa, where most of the human cargo except for us wrens was to disembark. We were looking forward to the extra sleeping space when told there was a change of plan. Apparently the logistics of war meant we were needed more urgently in Ceylon than South Africa. So we were given a few minutes, in that crowded cabin, to pack and get ready for disembarkation.

The 'wrennery' in Mombasa to which we were taken was the only naval establishment I ever found myself in that was feminine, with the fragrance of fresh flowers. We were told to be ready to leave there at short notice, but after a few days the plan was changed again. As there were no troopships due to sail east, we would remain in Mombasa for Christmas. No sooner had we unpacked, however, than it was decided we could join a commissioned naval cruiser, HMS Chitral, about to depart for Colombo, so we hurriedly packed again.

EASTWARD HO!

For legal reasons, its taking a dozen wrens on board meant we had to be designated members of the ship's company, not troops in transit – and we were the first women ever to serve on board a Royal Navy ship at war. To keep us busy we had lessons in nautical subjects – such as plumbing the depths, knotting and splicing, piping calls and the science of torpedoes – and I always enjoyed learning new things.

War or no war, Christmas on board was a feast of upper-class Victorian proportions, and we wrens were given a full Christmas lunch. Then, being the only women on board, we were invited by naval officers to the wardroom for all the same again in the evening! As for the plentiful alcohol available, I had never even heard of most of the spirits, so had to try a little of each. It is the only time in my life I have ever been really drunk.

Now that we were far beyond the reach of the Luftwaffe and German submarines ('U-boats'), I imagined we were in no danger as we sailed across the Indian Ocean.

However, although our voyage encountered no enemy action, six weeks later, in a five-ship convoy, the SS Khedive Ismail – a passenger liner requisitioned as a troopship – was carrying the next batch of wrens likewise from Mombasa to Colombo when, approaching Colombo, it was tragically struck by two Japanese torpedoes, and the boiler exploded. The ship took only 36 seconds to sink. Of the 1,511 people on board, 1,297, including seventeen of the nineteen wrens, were drowned or eaten by sharks.

Those of us on board HMS Chitral were lucky enough to be spared even the intimation of any such possibility – though we might have wondered why we kept veering over the Equator, as the Commander informed us we were, and seasoned sailors threatened us with the traditional crossing-the-line ceremony.

HMS Chitral

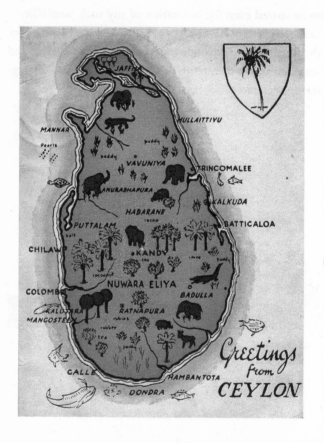

Greetings from CEYLON

CHAPTER THREE
OUTPOST OF EMPIRE

ON the last morning of 1943, HMS Chitral dropped anchor in Colombo, and we disembarked. The wrennery we were taken to was St Peter's, a former boarding school, probably for the sons (or daughters) of rich colonists.

I was raring to explore Colombo and have fun, but the wrens were allowed out only with a white male escort, so we newcomers, knowing nobody, had to stay in while the veteran Colombo wrens went off to New Year parties and dances with their escorts – who had to sign for them like parcels.

A day or two later, I was taken (by truck) to the wireless room in the naval headquarters, and assigned to a bay with a fixed service from Colombo to Australia – a country which, to conceal the real destination of signals, was often used as a go-between for onward transmission.

PRIORITY

I well remember a top-priority designated message being rushed to my wireless bay by two petty-officers on 12th February 1944. The signal had to be tapped out immediately on my Morse key, and one of the two men who brought it to me said he should take over my bay for sending it, as it was a very serious message. But I retorted 'It's my bay, so I must send it'. And I did.

The text being in the four-figure secret code of the day, I knew nothing about its content, which I now know was the death-dealing sinking that day of the troopship SS Khedive Ismail, steaming towards Colombo, as broached in Chapter 2. The total number of lives lost made it the third worst shipping disaster of the Second World War, but there remained an official news blackout on the tragedy for the next forty years.

The seventeen wrens whose lives were so tragically sacrificed are commemorated in St Mary le Strand – the ancient church dedicated to the WRNS on a street island in the Strand, London. Their names are engraved on its Paschal candlestick. The verger there told me that prayers are said for them every year on the Sunday closest to the anniversary. I responded that it would do them no good, but I was glad they were still remembered.

Throughout the rest of the war, which was to hold out for another twenty months, I saw no other top-priority signal. Only after the armistice did I see another – which took precedence over all other serious news. It was in plain language. Believe it or not, it read 'Splice the Mainbrace' – meaning that, in celebration of the Allied victory over Japan, male sailors above the age of 18 were to be allowed double their daily issue of rum, while wrens (who were normally given beer instead of rum) were to be allowed a single tot of the rum. Wars ordain their own sense of priorities.

In Colombo, I located the nearest Catholic church

– quite a big one, with an automatic peal of the Lourdes hymn ringing out every quarter of an hour, day and night! The church was a couple of miles distant from our wrennery, and to get to early Mass I used to go out on to the roadway, where rickshaw runners were sleeping in their rickshaws, and shake one of them awake to take me to the church, for a rupee.

I soon had a Royal Airforce man friend who happened to be on good terms with a local café owner, through whom I got to know a number of Sinhalese and Burgher locals. One of them, Phyllis – the wife of the café owner – herself owned a flower-shop next to the café. She planned to take her three-year-old daughter up-country for a convalescent fortnight in a vacation bungalow owned by her family, and asked me if I would like to go with them. As I was due for some leave, I asked the WRNS for permission to do so, and they gave it.

The procedure was that any service personnel going to stay with locals should be given a ration of rice to take with them, and, loaded with a sack of it, I took a rickshaw to the flower-shop on my way. As it happened, my hostess had already packed a good supply of food for the holiday, having taken rice from her husband's café, so she simply gave him my sack of rice in part replacement.

UP-COUNTRY

We travelled to Diyatalawa by train, and an RAF officer who was a fellow passenger took a shine to me. He got Phyllis to show him on his large-scale map exactly where our bungalow was situated – the only building in its valley – so that he could fly there a few days later to see me. But the day he came we ate such a big curry lunch that we both slept through the loud noise of his plane (as we were later told), circling the valley in an apparent search for a possible flat landing site – which did not exist.

It was a wonderful holiday. One delightful memory of it is being given a well-bath, which meant women servants dousing me with buckets of really cold water from the well – exhilarating in the tropical heat.

Less delightful, however, is the memory of one adventure when, visiting Banderawella (the next station), I forgot about the tropical lack of twilight and was disoriented by the sudden darkness. Unable to find my way back to the station, but coming upon part of the railway, I decided to walk along the railway line to get back to Diyatalawa. Coming to a dark tunnel with no footpath besides it, I had to feel my way through it from sleeper to sleeper. It was a relief to reach the tunnel's end eventually, but then a train passed me, and I suddenly realised that if had come a minute earlier I would have been crushed by it in the tunnel.

I had come out on the wrong hillside, with no footpath down to our valley, and this meant I had to scramble down through the undergrowth. Halfway down, I shouted out and was heard by the people in our bungalow, so a manservant came out with a lamp. Looking out next morning, I found I had narrowly missed a vertical rocky precipice – not to mention venomous snakes in the bushes – and thanked my guardian angel (!) for guiding me.

Diyatalawa was completely unspoiled at that time – but

within a year it acquired a built-up services' leave camp, which was a general bounty but spoilt it for me.

On returning to Colombo at the end of the holiday I was summoned to see a senior WRNS officer, who told me grimly that I had to report to the local police. It seemed that during my absence there had been a random inspection of the café, where a sack of rice marked as naval provisions had been found and confiscated. The café owner, facing a criminal interrogation, had given my name as the source of it. Though the true explanation that I was able to give to the police was accepted by them, they never returned the rice!

Then, without any reason being given, I was told by a WRNS officer that I was to be transferred from Colombo to Trincomalee (on the north-east coast). I was loath to leave Colombo, having made lots of friends there, and it happened that there was another wren telegraphist whose boyfriend was in Trinco and who would therefore like to swap with me. The communications officer having no objection to this, I sought an interview with a senior WRNS officer to arrange it.

However, she said my transfer to Trincomalee had already been finalised, and it was too late to change it. The reason for it, she told me, was that I was to replace a wren who had to leave Trinco 'for a very special reason'. I was therefore put on a train for the long journey by myself.

TRINCOMALEE

Trinco was a hotbed of malaria, and as well as having the usual mosquito-nets to protect us at night we were issued with elasticated sleeves and leggings to put on in the evenings – except, that is, for New Year's Eve, when mosquitoes were apparently not expected to bite.

After a few days, I got to know who the wren was that I had replaced and who her friends had been, and I asked them what the 'special reason' was for her transfer. Surprised by my question, they said she had been told that it was to replace me – and that I had to be transferred from Columbo 'for a very special reason'. Presumably, however innocent I might have been, the mere fact of my being questioned by the Ceylon police was guilt in the eyes of the WRNS.

I was told that there were 800 times as many male sailors in Trinco as there were wrens, and we were rather expected to go to at least one dance a week while the men were lucky to obtain a ticket for one a year. At one dance, I remember two men coming to blows over which one of them had asked me first for a dance, so I went off and danced with someone else.

The Trincomalee harbour being one of the largest natural harbours in the world, the Royal Navy had as many as sixty capital ships stationed there – an impossible number today.

We worked '24-about' on a four day rota, the longest workday comprising the Forenoon Watch (8am to midday), the two Dog Watches together (4pm to 8pm) and the Morning Watch (2am to 8am). When I was on the Morning Watch I used to choose the time of the sunrise for my twenty-minute break, go out on to the jetty that jutted into the harbour and stand there watching the sun come up in a blaze of colour.

Another natural pageant was the multiple forked lightning in a tropical storm, while the torrential monsoon rain afforded me and my hut-mates an invigorating shower as we stood in the nude outside our hut – with a lookout for any men in the offing.

At the end of a dry spell, one of the other dormitory huts caught fire and was destroyed within minutes, the thatched walkways between the huts threatening to spread the fire. After that, the palm-leaf thatch of the walkways was removed as a precaution, making the countless small creatures that lived in it homeless. That evening, I felt something cold land on my bare foot, and looking down saw it was a big black scorpion, its tail already arching over to sting my leg. I managed to shake it off and phoned the armed guard to come and kill it, but it eluded us, and I had to crawl under my mosquito-net knowing that the scorpion, alive and angry, was still near my bed.

I was also involved in a number of accidents, of which I will describe just one – the most spectacular. Having been to the naval dockyard to collect my month's pay, I was on my way back along the harbour embankment when offered a lift in a small army truck. It had a Sinhalese driver and, in the passenger seat, an English soldier. In the back where I sat, was a crate of glass bottles.

I would never have accepted the lift had I known that the driver had only just learnt to drive and this was his first time out on the road. He decided to overtake a vehicle ahead of us, and began to do so – on the wrong side, which was the harbour side. The other vehicle moved in, leaving no space for us, and our driver, instead of braking, raised both hands from the steering wheel and cried 'My God!' – whereupon the truck, overturning, fell into the sea.

Instinctively, I put my arm up in front of my face, and a shard of glass cut my wrist. I was able to get to my feet with water almost up to my waist, and seeing a gang of Tamil labourers across the road called out to them to come over and help us. The soldier having fallen on a small rock, with the truck on top of him, the workmen lifted it off him and pulled him up on to the bank. They also dragged out the driver, who had no physical injuries but had apparently fainted from fright.

I had been clutching my paybook containing my month's salary in banknotes, and now placed it on the bank as I scrambled up and went on to the road to stop vehicles and get them to take us to hospital.

The Tamils had been very brave, running over the glass-strewn path on their bare feet, but one of them stole my paybook and money. Though we all survived, the soldier's pelvis was fractured and my wrist required several surgical stitches. I still have the scar, 75 years later, and am glad that I shielded my face. To add insult to injury, I was penalised for losing my paybook, which was no doubt sold as a pass-muster passport.

Soon afterwards I formed a close but secret friendship with a Sinhalese army officer named Filo Fernando – secret, because it was the ultimate sin for a wren to associate with a brown-skinned 'native'. Ironically, within two years of the end of the war, Filo was awarded an OBE.

WAR NEWS

The war having turned in our favour by 1945 (largely thanks to the Red Army), a British General Election was planned. Having passed my 21st birthday, I was entitled to claim a proxy vote, and I filled in the form with my father's name as proxy. Writing home, I said that while I knew nothing about the local candidates, I rather fancied a post-war Labour government under the unwarlike Clement Attlee. Afterwards mum told me that Dad had grumbled on Election Day that it was a waste of his time going to the polling-station to cast a Conservative vote on his own behalf and a Labour one on mine. But he was too upright not to do so.

I was the first person in Trinco to know that the war in Europe was over, as I happened to receive the Admiralty signal that read 'Tomorrow Tuesday 8 May will be VE Day'. The repeat of it began, and I shouted out the news. Within seconds men were pulling out the bottles of celebratory beer they had hidden away for this moment.

On 15 August, prior to going on the Forenoon Watch (from 8 am), I set off at 6 am down the inner harbour road to thumb a lift to the Catholic church for Mass – as, being the feast of the Assumption (i.e. the doctrinal assumption of the BVM into Heaven), it was a Holiday of Obligation. But there were unusual traffic jams, and, realising I could not reach the church in time, I changed direction and went straight to naval headquarters. On the way, I noticed ships in the harbour being dressed with celebratory flags.

Arriving in the wireless room early for my duty, I quizzed the leader of the previous watch as to what was happening.

He told me that Japan had surrendered, and I asked to be shown the Admiralty text announcing it.

It had always appalled me that, in 1918 on and after 11th November, many men were still being maimed or killed because there were combatants on both sides unaware that the armistice had been signed. Indeed, it is alleged that some over-zealous officers deliberately kept the information from them.

Therefore, now that Japan had surrendered, I resolved to spread the word. So when the leader of my watch arrived and assigned me to the low-frequency Port Wave, I asked him whether the ships at sea would have been informed that the war was over. 'They will know soon enough when they get into harbour' was the reply. 'No, that is not soon enough,' I objected. 'I want to let them know now.'

To do so, he said, I would need to obtain permission from the 'Baker Charlie Oboe' – Base Communications Officer – whose arrival was expected at 9 am. So I looked out for him and, waylaying him, said 'I want to let the ships at sea know the war is over'. Obviously overwhelmed by a surge of peacetime responsibilities, he pushed me aside, snapping 'Do what you like! Do what you like!'.

Taking that as permission, tongue-in-cheek, I immediately went to the Port Wave bay and tapped out this message on its Morse key (in those days it was all manual Morse): 'CQ' (meaning all ships), 'V' (from), my call-sign on that service (which I still remember!), and 'PL' (plain language), followed by the words 'The war against Japan is over' – then 'IMI' for repetition.

I realised that it was unlikely the war was officially over, no armistice treaty having been signed, but I reasoned it would be unconscionable to continue bombarding a foe who had already surrendered. My jumping the peaceful gun could have got me into trouble, but no-one in charge apparently noticed what I had done off my own bat, so I got away with it.

A few hours later, still on Port Wave, I was amazed to pick up this signal from another imperial base: 'The follow-ing has been read from Trincomalee', then my own text – as though it were official!

It remains one of my proudest boasts, and I like to think that my enterprise may have actually saved lives. Further-more, it gave me the realisation that an unimportant individ-ual like me could gain a wide influence if one felt strongly enough about something, so that seventeen years later I was able to take part in direct action with the Committee of 100, set up by Bertrand Russell as a less law-abiding off-shoot of the Campaign for Nuclear Disarmament.

I no longer saw blind obedience as a virtue, nor regarded lying as necessarily immoral. Other things might be more important. Though truth always remained my overriding moral principle, it no longer meant verbal strictness, un-less for general information or involved in anyone's right to know. A classical ethical dilemma is whether one should give a truthful answer to authorities on the trail of an escaping fugitive – but that must depend on likely consequences, not on the law nor on a scrupulous reply.

ABSENT WITHOUT LEAVE

I struck up a friendship with a Leading Wren (halfway to a Petty Officer) named Pauline. It was mainly based on our mutual enjoyment of illicit expeditions. Pauline, who was quite knowledgeable about Ceylon, told me that its ancient capital Anaradhapura was near enough for us to get there and back in a day, and as it boasted ruins said to be 3,000 years old it would be a shame not to visit them. It required special permission for us to travel outside the Trincomalee area, and we would never get permission for such a jaunt, so the only course was to leave without going through the regulating office to sign ourselves out. This we did, and had a great day. Needless to say, we used false names. There was a slightly scary incident when a man began following us, but Pauline had a simple way of dealing with it. Physically strong, she turned and punched him, and he beat a hasty retreat.

A couple of days after the Japanese surrender, Pauline told me about a spectacular procession taking place every evening for the next week in Kandy – which was much further afield. It was then announced that naval personnel were to celebrate the victory over Japan with an extra day's leave, as well as 'splicing the mainbrace'. If Pauline and I were to choose the same day off, and if it came between two normal rest days, we could have three clear days' holiday together, which would enable us to take the challenging trip to Kandy, without clearance.

The promised procession was a religious event called the Perahera, in which Buddha's supposed tooth was taken from the Temple of the Tooth and carried around Kandy in a gilded howdah on elephant back. Normally it was an annual event, but it had been suspended for the duration of the war. The armistice meant it was now being revived, celebrating the victory over Japan as well as the Buddhist commemoration – and a huge number of caparisoned elephants was promised in attendance. This was unmissable.

It did not occur to me at the time that the Perahera was remarkably similar to the annual Corpus Christi event back home, when the consecrated disc-shaped host was carried in a gold monstrance from the tabernacle in Catholic churches through the streets of south-east London. As a small child I used to participate in the local procession, wearing a white dress and veil and strewing rose-petals in the path of the revered biscuit.

GETTING AWAY WITH IT

Pauline was a past-master at getting away with things. Her first trick was to look official – for instance, by walking purposefully – and when we set out for our big adventure we each carried a brief-case as a prop.

To get to Kandy we decided to take a plane from a nearby airfield to Colombo, and hitch-hike from there. Not, of course, to pay for the flight: everything in Pauline's book was free. Entering the control tower, she addressed the man in charge breathlessly, as though it were a matter of life and death: 'We need the next plane to Colombo'. He said there was one leaving almost immediately, not to Colombo itself but to Ratmalana, which was close, and when the young pilot came in, told him 'You have to take these two wrens with you' – as though it was official.

It was a small (four-seater) plane, with no other passengers, no co-pilot and no communication from air to ground. When we were airborne, Pauline slid into the co-pilot seat and began playing with the controls, much to the pilot's amusement. After a while, not to be outdone, I changed places with her. We must have flown out of our way, as I saw the sea below us. Then the pilot took over again, to take us back on course and land the plane.

When we stepped out on the tarmac, an official came running towards us, and Pauline hissed at me 'Look important!' She said to the official 'We are from Trincomalee, and we need a transport into Colombo'. Without any explanation, we were given one, which took us to a friend of mine and he put us on the right road to get a lift to Kandy.

In an army truck, we approached Kandy just before nightfall, and I asked Pauline where we would be spending the night. 'We are part of the Navy, so the Navy has to look after us' was her reply – as though we were within our rights. She asked the truck driver to drop us at the wrennery beside Lord Louis Mountbatten's headquarters, a couple of miles before Kandy.

Pauline then went in and told the duty WRNS officer 'We have missed our transport back to Trincomalee, and would be grateful if you could put us up for the night.' The officer complained that it was most irregular, but as two of her wrens were away on leave we could use their beds. I then said 'As we happen to be here, and apparently there is an interesting event in Kandy this evening, perhaps we could join a group of your wrens going there.' 'We are not allowing any of them to go – it is far too dangerous', she replied.

Therefore, after claiming our beds, we had to creep out past the regulating office and hitch a lift into Kandy. The procession had already started, with the dressed elephants reflected in the lake, and it was breath-taking. At the end, we decided to follow the elephants where they were to be unloaded, and there we were picked up by two American soldiers, who eventually drove us back to our night quarters.

On arriving back in Trinco 24 hours later, I discovered that my absence overnight (but not Pauline's) had been rumbled by the duty officer, who included my hut in her rounds, and the lies told her by my friends there on my behalf failed to convince her. Then the Kandy officer who had given us the beds for the night apparently phoned Trinco to say that two Trinco wrens had turned up there. Happily the phone call was answered not by the duty officer but by her wren assistant, who did not tell her about the call. Putting two and two together, the wren went over to a book in which extra duties were recorded, opened the book, and said 'Oh, that's all right – Wren Smoker is on extra duty at HQ this evening'. She then closed the book, and the duty officer left it at that.

However, my general disregard for the minutiae of naval discipline was not always so lucky, and I wondered how it would be officially assessed when my war-service came to an end. So when, back home, I received my discharge papers, I turned to the word 'Conduct', and was pleasantly surprised to see it given the rating 'Good' – until I discovered that everyone else scored 'Exemplary'.

Pauline's amazing ability to get away with everything was down to her supreme self-confidence; her seniority to me both in age and rank obviously contributed to this, but the basic factor, I am sure, is being 'spoilt' as a child.

I would define my social background as lower-middle-class but Pauline's as middle-middle-class. After the war she invited me to her home for a day with her widowed mother, who was bereft of servants for the first time. The mother prepared our two-course lunch and was noticeably embarrassed to have to rise from the table after the main course to clear it away and fetch the pudding from the kitchen. In all seriousness she asked me 'How do other people manage without a butler?'

DEMOBILISATION

Peace having been declared on all fronts, all of us on active service were soon on our way home. The homebound ship I boarded was just as crowded as the one that had carried me out East back in 1943, but without the German bombardments or any potential Japanese torpedoes. I recall writing some light verses for the ship's magazine, and that is my only memory about the voyage.

Wartime experiences had at least opened up to me the wider world and its realities, but could I not have learnt such things without the global horrors of war?

Calamitously, to quote the Matthew gospel (24/6): 'Of wars and rumours of wars...the end is not yet'. It does indeed seem that each succeeding generation has to learn the same lessons over and over again (if at all). Equally calamitous, and not disconnected, is the survival of dogmatic religion. Though traditional Christianity is (thank God!) on its last legs in Britain, it has been overtaken by innumerable new faiths, from Scientology to that of the practitioners of child exorcism – many of them even worse, both psychologically and socially, than the faith I was born into. In the same way, immigrant Islam has become increasingly misogynist and is breeding 'radicalised' jihadist (that is, terrorist) 'martyrs' against the infidel West.

The untenable belief that most religions have in common is in the immortality of an individual 'soul' – at least for themselves, the destined few – while some still cling to the execrable medieval acceptance of eternal damnation for heretics and apostates.

Freethinker, 1950

CHAPTER FOUR
VOCATION

THE NUNS at my secondary school tried to prime me as a future member of their religious order; but teaching nuns and those engaged in other social work are not properly called nuns at all. Strictly speaking, they are 'sisters' – or, as Aunty Isabel scathingly called them, 'half-nuns'. The life to which I aspired was that of a proper nun – such as a Carmelite – in a contemplative community, devoted to prayer, not social work. But Mum said I should wait until I was 18 before 'entering'.

Nine years later she said the same thing to Paula – who, on reaching the age of 18, accordingly became a 'half-nun', choosing the Good Shepherd order – which she eventually helped to modernise. She always made a joke of everything, and I remember her laughing at the fact that before her time the nuns had actually used the term 'fallen women'. In Ireland, however, the Good Shepherd sisterhood was still mired in those cruel Dark Ages.

'SISTER' PAULA

After qualifying as an educational psychologist, she was appointed principal (the youngest and most progressive) of one of the governmental Approved Schools, to which the criminal courts sentenced delinquent girls. She allowed its inmates unprecedented independence, finally living in pairs in flats of their own. She then oversaw the dissolution of the school and sale of its valuable Wiltshire site. Later she was put in charge of the Chepstow camp of Vietnamese refugees (the so-called 'boat people'), with responsibility for their learning English, finding jobs, securing accommodation and so on.

Once or twice Paula accompanied the Catholic chaplain of Holloway Prison when he visited Moors Murder accomplice Myra Hindley there. Asked whether, like Lord Longford, she accepted Myra's professed religious revival as genuine, she pulled a face and said she thought it was merely a 'try-on' for parole.

On one occasion, when I arranged to meet her in central London, she arrived on a motor-bike, helmeted, wearing trousers and a scarlet top – though the then pope, John-Paul II, had reportedly urged nuns to go back to their traditional habit. When I mockingly reminded her of this, she replied 'I will ask him whether he wears his mitre on the ski slopes.' And when she celebrated her silver jubilee in the order, she announced that, rather than receive gifts of a dozen brief-cases, she would like to have the cash to go on a pilgrimage to Rome. She then did so, accompanied by a younger member of the order, her closest friend. (They actually spent one or two days in Rome, followed by a week or so sunbathing in Sorrento.)

However, she remained in the Good Shepherd order till her death, from cancer at the early age of 58 – having done

Paula (Sister Thomas More)

a lot in the wake of the Vatican Council to liberalise the life-style of her fellow nuns, as well as succouring former delinquents, Vietnamese boat people and others. She was given a huge funeral in Liverpool, and a road in London (Thomas More Way) was later named after her – in her religious name, though in fact she had finally reverted to that of her birth.

RELIGIOUS SEXUALITY

A young man who had asked Paula out when she was in her teens told me later that she explained her refusal by saying she was going to be a 'bride of Christ'—which is the designation that nuns have historically been given.

Genuine sexual feeling usually underlies a young

woman's 'vocation' to become a nun, and probably a gay man's to become a monk. The focus, Jesus Christ, is known among intellectuals as 'the ghostly lover' – rather like a child's imaginary friend. Though mainly Catholic, it has not been exclusively so. For instance, Annie Besant, after becoming an atheist, related how, in her devout teenage Protestantism, she had indulged in fantasies of being martyred for her faith, inspired by Foxe's *Book of Martyrs*. And I suspect that similar heroic fantasies may motivate individual Muslim terrorists.

The erotic religious fantasies of the 16th-century Saint Teresa of Avila, as she herself described them, were graphically depicted in Nigel Wingrove's film *Visions of Ecstasy*, in which her conjured lesbianesque *alter ego* makes a threesome with Christ on the cross and herself, blood dripping from a hand nailed to the cross.

Her latter-day namesake (Mother Teresa of Calcutta) probably had similar visions. She welcomed suffering, as a share in Christ's supposed suffering on the cross, and for that reason banned any pain-killer stronger than an aspirin from her institutions for the dying – though the patients, many in agony, were not even Christian but mainly Hindu. In her own terminal illness, however, she stayed in a Western-style hospital, not one of her own hospices.

I remember indulging in religio-sexual fantasies myself in my religious teens, and my first paramour was naturally Jesus, the ghostly lover.

Though my masochistic feelings never led to the extent of self-harm, my teenage love affair with Jesus means I can understand the underlying emotional pull that may involve self-harm, as well as its causing young people to take up the religious life in their sexually highly-charged youth. When their emotions settle down in later years, they must often regret their religious vocation, and I think this is what is meant by 'the dark night of the soul'. In the end they become used to it, as most people do in non-religious boring jobs.

The fact that very few middle-aged inmates who feel trapped in their convents and monasteries will then 'leap over the wall' (to use Monica Baldwin's phrase) is down to practical considerations. Not only have the fellow members of their community become their family, as in marriage, but they have no home of their own outside to go to, nor any other possessions. Any money they had before entering would have been handed over as an irrecoverable dowry, and they do not even own the clothes they are wearing.

One day, visiting Paula when she was hospitalised with 'deep depression' (while, paradoxically, joking and laughing all the time), I asked her if she would like to leave her religious order, since the family would no doubt be willing to help her do so. 'Oh no', she replied; 'the order would like to kick me out, but I don't want to leave.'

I once knew a woman who had been a Dominican nun for nine years, and she told me that her convent had been a hotbed of lesbianism, in which the novice-mistress enjoyed the first pick of each wave of new entrants, called 'postulants'.

As for my own mature sexuality, I have always been attracted to people near the middle of the somatic spectrum – butch girls and rather effeminate men – but as for intimacy, I could take it or leave it. In fact, I now regard most physical intimacy, including kisses, as both undignified and unhygienic. Even shaking hands is known to be a major cause of colds, as it transfers germs from hand to hand; the next time you put your hand to your face you breathe in the germs. I prefer the modern practice of hugging, though I would never initiate it.

In recent years, a new question has appeared at the end of survey forms and other questionnaires, asking for one's sexual orientation. (In some cases this may be relevant, but very rarely.) There are usually boxes to be ticked for each of the letters 'LGBT' (Lesbian, Gay, Bisexual, Trans), as the supposedly exhaustive alternatives to Heterosexual, but a few extra letters are gradually being added, such as 'A' (Asexual), 'Q' (Questioning), and so on. Incidentally, I wonder how monks and nuns, being vowed to perpetual chastity, answer this question.

Recently, a representative of the housing association of which I am a tenant was filling in a survey form on my behalf, and sure enough that question was included – though I cannot see what relevance it bears to my tenancy. When I hesitated before replying, the young woman who was ticking the boxes at my prompting pointed out the final option: 'Prefer not to say'. But that seemed to imply shame or prudery – neither of which I felt, though it might be of help to the nuns and monks. I told the woman that I was one of the many who do not experience enjoyment in an intimate physical contact with others, and suggested she should simply write down the appropriate word 'Asexual', since no 'A' box was included on the form. She looked doubtful, but did so.

Just as, decades ago, it was important for gays to 'come out', in order to repudiate the false belief that homosexuality was rare and abnormal, so, perhaps, it is similarly important today for asexuals to stand up and be counted – though, unlike the case with gays, it is generally unwanted pity they evoke rather than hostility. Even the label Asexual, however, could be subdivided, as it can mean either self-sexual (masturbating) or simply under-sexed, or even steadfastly asexual by choice.

JANET

When I came home from Ceylon at the end of 1945, my youngest sister was six – and that is when she made up her mind about her life's vocation. She was going to be a magician.

Galvanised by the skill of a member of the Magic Circle at the parish children's Christmas party, she decided there and then – partly, no doubt, to outdo her older siblings – that her goal in life would be to learn the secrets of show-business deception. Though Dad told her it could well become a hobby but not an earned living, she never gave up her dream.

At the age of 13, feeling she was making no headway with it, she wrote for advice to David Nixon, the foremost professional magician of the day, who was a TV pioneer. He replied, giving her the address of the London Society of Magicians, which, he said, ran a junior section. A keen member of it for the next five years, she was then forced to leave – because of her sex.

On reaching the age of 18, male students automatically went up to the LSM senior section or auditioned for the Magic Circle, but women, of course, were not acceptable as magicians, only magicians' assistants. Janet therefore visited the Wardour Street emporium of magic, run by the magicians' magician, Ken Brooke. His rough Yorkshire manner frightened her at first, but he had a great gift of humour as well as showmanship, and became not only her one-to-one coach for magic performance but the most significant person in her life.

In 1982 feminism finally knocked at the door of the London Society of Magicians, and Janet went in. From 1984 to 1987 she was its secretary and from 1987 to 1989 its president. But the Magic Circle continued to ostracise women.

Meanwhile, Janet entered international magic contests, and if Magic Circle members were also competing she determined to beat them – and did. At long last, in 1991, the Magic Circle decided to admit women, and Janet was among them. In 1994, she was the first woman elected to the council of the Magic Circle. Despite ill health she still gives shows for charity.

Women's status in the Abrahamic religions has yet to catch up even with the Magic Circle.
Religious ritual – especially transubstantiation in the Catholic Mass, when magic words spoken by the priest are actually believed to turn bread and wine into the body and blood of Jesus – has a lot in common with mental magic, if not with sleight of hand. So it seemed to me that Janet's expertise as a magician should be a stumbling block against belief,

Janet was one of the first women to join
the Magic Circle

yet she has remained a life-long Catholic and, moreover, a
parish activist. I therefore asked her one day: 'Do you really
believe in transubstantiation?' 'Oh no', she said; 'I've never
believed in that'.

Since it is a core dogma of the Church, how, I asked her,
could she remain a Catholic and not believe in it? 'It's not
believing', she replied; 'it's belonging.' And I realised that for
many religionists it is indeed simply a matter of belonging.

That would not work for me, though, since I could never
feel I 'belonged' in any organisation which impugned my

reason. It must therefore depend on the relative strengths of one's emotion and reason – which reveals an essential difference in temperament between Janet and myself.

When children ask their RE teachers 'Is it true, or just pretend?', they are often given the worst possible answer: 'It is true for some people'. Since a factual statement must be either true or false, not both together – that answer is irrational, and therefore anti-educational. A more honest answer, while still non-committal, would be 'Some people think it is true, other people don't.'

APOSTASY

Had it not been for the outbreak of war before I reached the age that Mum would let me join a religious order, I might well have taken the same route as Paula. As it was, wartime naval service in multi-creedal Ceylon helped dilute my indoctrinated faith. It took another four years, however, to turn my increasing doubts into certitude – on the apostatic side.

On holiday in Paris in 1948, I made a point of visiting a convent in Rue du Bac, having read that it housed the miraculously preserved corpse of a former Mother Superior. A nun admitted me and took me to their chapel, where, to my amazement, I found that the glass-sided coffin on the left of the altar was matched by another on the right, and the two women's faces beyond the glass looked waxed. The second body, I was told, was that of another holy nun, but I could not help thinking that two such miracles in one small convent was at least one too many. It may have helped to weaken my already flagging Catholicism.

I reached my life-stance verdict at midday on 5th November 1949 – which sounds like a sudden conversion, like St Paul's on the road to Damascus, but was in fact the culmination of years of reading and thinking.

There was I, that Saturday morning, standing in our local public library by the religion and philosophy shelves, reaching for one book after another – all of them books that I had already studied. Approaching my decisive moment, I felt impelled to check out particular arguments. And it was the apostasy arguments that won the conclusive battle. I said to myself 'I am no longer a Catholic.'

Aware that it was a major turning-point in my life, I looked up at the library clock on the wall, and saw it was exactly midday.

The reason that the final step had to be instantaneous was the Catholic claim of papal infallibility. Though, as an article of faith, this dated only from the 19th century, it endorsed the whole Catholic doctrinal package, which meant one could not pick and choose so as to keep the faith, as Protestants might. There was no halfway house for me: it had to be all or nothing. Choosing Catholicism would mean that I had to accept, to the letter, every doctrine of the Church – even to the absurdity of transubstantiation. Choosing apostasy therefore had to be sudden and total.

So it was not until the age of 26 that, after years of mental turmoil, I was able to overcome the conditioning of my Catholic childhood. And to me that meant not only the whole of Christianity but, indeed, the whole of religion.

It is amazing that I took so long for my innate reason

to dare challenge theological authority, but not only had I
been born into the faith; all my upbringing was designed
to bolster it. The doubts I pondered were always mere details; never the entire package. I well remember in my early
twenties reminding myself that many intellectuals accepted
doctrinal Catholicism – so who was I to question it? Two of
the English writers whom I admired, G K Chesterton and
Graham Greene, were actually converts – so did not even
have my inborn excuse!

Since I was always literal-minded, the idea of theological
metaphors cut no ice with me, any more than the idea, all
those years earlier, of Father Christmas as a metaphor; so it
was not possible for me to simply move on to a less stringent
form of religion. Metaphor is fine if it is honest metaphor, not
masquerading as reality. (It is like the honest deception of
show-business magic as opposed to the dishonesty practised
by Uri Geller – a competent magician from the Israeli Magic
Circle who chose to feign supernatural powers.)

To 'come out' at home about my conversion (perver-
sion?) was more difficult than it had been to confront my
mother about Father Christmas. Since my parents were not
in this case wilful deceivers, but themselves irredeemable
victims, I was loathe to upset them – not to mention possibly
having to find somewhere else to live.

On Sundays I therefore left the house at the right hour as
though to attend the last Mass of the morning, and usually
spent the time in the local park. One Sunday, there was a
rainstorm, and I ran for the same shelter as my brother John,
who, having been to an early Mass, was playing football in

the park. By that time, of course, he had reached the age of reason, and it took only one look at me for him to put two and two together. He could not get home quick enough to let my parents know I had not been to Mass.

Needless to say, I admitted it, and told them I was no longer a Catholic. My mother's response was to say that she would have to ask me to leave home, as I would otherwise be a bad influence on the younger members of the family. But I took my time looking for somewhere else to live, and eventually she relented and gave me the use of the top floor of the house.

In addition to books, one of my stimulants to rational thought was attending philosophical lectures – in particular, those at the Ethical Church (Stanton Coit's name for the Ethical Union's headquarters) in Bayswater. In those days such meetings were advertised inexpensively at the back of the *New Statesman*, and whenever the charismatic H J Blackham was named as the speaker I would cross London to hear him. Not that he was easy: I always had to look up a few words in the dictionary when I got home! But he made me think.

GLOBALISATION

Unknown to me at the time were Blackham's far-reaching plans for the global spread of pragmatic humanism – a word which he was responsible for gradually establishing (in our sense) in this country.

Disliking the religious decor of the Ethical Church, inherited from Stanton Coit and owned by the Ethical Union

The humanist philosopher, H J Blackham

together with West London Ethical Society, he got rid of its statues and sold the building. He invested the proceeds of sale in a large house in Prince of Wales Terrace, Kensington, as the new headquarters of the Ethical Union – which he later renamed the British Humanist Association.

His vision, however, went far beyond that. At first he had taken steps to join forces with the World Union of

Freethinkers, but did not really see eye-to-eye with them. The progressive humanist movement in Holland seemed to be more on his wavelength. After the war, therefore, as European travel became possible again, he contacted the Dutch humanist leader, Jaap van Praag, suggesting an international humanist conference for the purpose of setting up a permanent global humanist organisation. Taking place in Amsterdam in 1952, with a manifesto in support of reason, freedom of thought and personal liberty combined with social responsibility, the conference founded the International Humanist & Ethical Union.

For the operation of its own first conference, which was to take place in London, I volunteered to do secretarial work, which brought me closer to the three executives whose names began with 'B' – Burrell, Burnett, and, of course, Harold Blackham.

Today Harold's brain-child, IHEU, with 34 full organisational members and innumerable associates and supporters, is highly respected throughout the world as an effective non-religious mission for human rights.

Not only was Harold my mentor; decades later, he became a close friend. I asked him once to name his favourite philosopher, and his unhesitating reply was Santayana, the liberal materialist. Harold occasionally treated me to lunch at the National Liberal Club, of which he was a life member, and, among more serious activities, we enjoyed a pleasurable day-trip on the Orient Express. Later I was to organise his 100th birthday party at Conway Hall, and he did not die until a few weeks before his 106th birthday in 2009.

CIVVY STREET

Some careers advice on discharge from war service might have been expected, but if there was any available I knew nothing about it – only that the government undertook to meet the cost of whatever vocational training one required, together with a moderate living allowance while it lasted.

I was unwilling to go back to my pre-service job of insurance clerk, and of course there was no call in Civvy Street for my one acquired skill of manual Morse. I therefore needed to acquire some new employable expertise, and I opted for a secretarial course. Not that I had any intention of becoming a secretary, but I saw shorthand-typing as a reliable marketable skill in case of need at any time, whatever else I might do.

Years later I learnt that one of my WRNS friends had opted, more ambitiously, to enrol in a university law course, with a view to becoming an affluent barrister. I thought perhaps I should have done likewise, especially as litigation was always an interest of mine – but my innate anarchism would hardly have been suited to life in the establishment. Anyway, I must say, in retrospect, that I have enjoyed the alternative life I have had.

The government-funded secretarial tuition, which was almost exclusively taken up by women, meant attending a six-month course in Holborn. In our penultimate week, the college principal came in and said he wanted each of us to write an essay on the Bretton Woods Agreement, which had established credit for international trade in the post-war world. Knowing next to nothing about the subject, I went to the public library to see how the newspapers and weekly journals had commented on it, then went home to write it up, and handed in my script. The following week, the principal returned with our essays and distributed them, commenting on each one. Mine he left till last. Then he asked me 'Did you write this yourself?' Indignantly I replied 'Of course I did!' 'Ten thousand a year for you!' he said, handing it back. (A really colossal salary at that time.)

Meanwhile, I was beginning to win small cash prizes in literary competitions, of which there were many more in the papers then than there are today, and I used several *noms-de-plume* for multiple entries. Later I was to set some of the *New Statesman* and *Spectator* competitions and judge them.

I was also stage-struck. While serving king and country in Trincomalee I had appeared in a ship's concert, and this led to my being offered the part of a schoolgirl in a joint services amateur-dramatic production of *The Housemaster* by Ian Hay. It gave me the opportunity to indulge in boisterous fun, and the glowing reviews I received for it turned my head. Back in Civvy Street, I therefore applied for a scholarship to the Royal Academy of Dramatic Art, where I was auditioned – unsurprisingly without success. Then a touring company offered me a job. But I suddenly realised it would probably entail such physical hardships as dossing in church halls, so I turned it down and instead joined the semi-professional Tavistock Repertory Company in Bloomsbury (later the oc-cupants of Canonbury Tower). People are amused when I tell them that one of the parts I played there was that of a Christian in Shaw's *Androcles and the Lion*! More beneficially, I was given some speech-training.

THE SHAW SOCIETY

When, in 1950, the Shaw Society advertised its reprint of a Shavian tract on 'Creative Evolution', I ordered a copy – whereupon the Society's London secretary, Eric Batson, invited me to one of their summer rambles. I joined the

New Look, 1948

Society (in Shaw's own lifetime), and a year later became a Life Member. (An astute actuarial move!)

Eric was a semi-professional actor, with Shavian productions under his belt and solo dramatic entertainments that he termed 'lecture recitals'. His day job, though, was that of librarian at the City Literary Institute. Without the benefit of tertiary education, he somehow knew where to find information on anything, and often carried out research for scholars. Decades before the electronic internet took over, he was a sort of walking internet.

As well as taking me to interesting places, introducing me to interesting people and often making me laugh, he taught me a lot. One lesson, which was to stand me in good stead during my later presidency of the National Secular Society, was about press releases.

When Shaw died and details of his will were published, its primary bequest for the promotion of a new phonetic alphabet for English was impertinently condemned by a number of celebrities (including, I remember, the actor Tyrone Power) – as though the great dramatist had no right to leave his money to such a public cause. At the Shaw Society's small AGM, I therefore proposed a pious motion about it, which was of course passed. At the end of the meeting, Eric suggested that if I were to write an introductory sentence to it, I could, on my way home, deliver the wording of my resolution to the news-desk of the Press Association in Fleet Street. I did so. The next morning, to my amazement, I was informed by my mother that I had been quoted in the early BBC radio news bulletins.

Though Shaw left a sizable fortune, his estate was plunged into debt for five years, due to the Inland Revenue demanding a huge sum in death duties, based on an unprecedented formula for valuing Shaw's copyrights, which he had never sold. A question was raised in the House of Commons about the abnormally avaricious formula used, but to no avail.

Shaw's executor, the Public Trustee, therefore put pressure on the Society of Authors, as his literary executor, to increase, by hook or by crook, royalties accruing to the estate, so that the debt to the Inland Revenue could be cleared. Only then could Shaw's will be implemented – or, at least, steps be taken to test the legal validity of his proposed phonetic alphabet trust. When a lucrative American offer was received to turn the play *Pygmalion* into a musical, the Public Trustee and the Society of Authors jumped at it – though Shaw had always refused it. But Moss Hart and H. M. Tennent demanded a lot for the high percentage they paid for the rights – including a clause in the contract to impose a total worldwide ban for the next ten years on Shaw's own play and film, so as to give the musical a clear unrivalled run.

Apparently it did not occur to the negotiators representing the proposed musical that, apart from the improbability of many of the potential customers for it choosing to buy tickets for the original play instead of the musical version, some theatre-goers might even have liked to have the opportunity to see both *Pygmalion* and *My Fair Lady* in the same week, for comparison.

The Shaw Society was naturally outraged by the ban, and

Eric set up the Not Bloody Likely Committee to oppose the iniquitous contract. Among the celebrities who supported us was Graham Greene, who publicly cancelled his membership of the Society of Authors in protest. But the ban on *Pygmalion* endured – not for ten years, but for twenty.

SOUTH PLACE ETHICAL SOCIETY

Prospecting a progressive hostel that advertised affordable single rooms for single people, I met a young resident, Douglas Lawson, who apparently fell for my red hair and curvaceous figure. An atheist and anarchist, he took me in 1951 to Conway Hall in Holborn, for a lecture by the famous anarchist Herbert Read.

At the bookstall (manned by Edwina Palmer), I saw that the building belonged to the South Place Ethical Society and that its secretary was Hector Hawton. His name was familiar to me as that of the author of *The Thinker's Handbook* – a work that I had already read with approbation. Deciding, therefore, there and then, that this Society must be where I belonged, I promptly joined it. The next year I followed my usual practice of becoming a Life Member – at about two percent of today's cost! So I have actually been a member of SPES (now renamed Conway Hall Ethical Society) for some 67 years – only three years short (so far) of the biblical life-span.

During that time I have served for many years on its General Committee (now the Board of Trustees), eventually as the Chairman, and, at different times, its Honorary Representative (like a president), a Holding Trustee (responsible for Conway Hall), its Editor, and from 1986 an Appointed Lecturer.

The title 'Appointed Lecturer' had been adopted at the beginning of the twentieth century to supersede 'Minister'. Now no more, Appointed Lecturers were called upon in my time to give about half the Sunday morning lectures (time-tabled as an alternative to religious services), with outside lecturers giving the other half on their specialist subjects. There is a memorial board in the foyer of Conway Hall listing all the Ministers and Appointed Lecturers from 1793—my name taking up the last space. (I am the only person who is still living, and the only woman on the whole list.)

I discovered in the early days of my membership that some of the elderly members on the General Committee were known as 'family members' – meaning that they had ancestors in the original congregation, with intermarriage, and that they themselves had attended the South Place Sunday School in the late 19th century.

On the 23rd September 2004, the 75th anniversary of the opening of Conway Hall was celebrated by a panel of speakers on which I was honoured to join Polly Toynbee, Richard Dawkins, and the cartoonist Martin Rowson. Two days later, Rowson's sweeping cartoon of the occasion appeared in *The Times*, and, though I was hardly flattered by my caricature, I was both amused and gratified by his description of me as 'the Queen Mum of Secularism'. Similarly the *Northern Echo* once described me as 'the militant martinet of the National Secular Society'.

One of the innumerable friendships I have forged over

SOUTH PLACE ETHICAL SOCIETY

MINISTERS		APPOINTED LECTURERS	
Rev ELHANAN WINCHESTER	1793-1794	Dr C E M JOAD	1941-1944
Rev WILLIAM VIDLER	1794-1816	PROFESSOR G W KEETON	1941-1952
Rev WILLIAM JOHNSON FOX MP	1817-1852	ARCHIBALD ROBERTSON	1944-1961
Rev HENRY IERSON	1853-1857	Dr W E SWINTON	1955-1961
Rev H N BARNETT	1858-1863	H J BLACKHAM	1965-2009
Dr MONCURE D CONWAY	1864-1884	RICHARD CLEMENTS OBE	1965-1988
Dr STANTON COIT	1888-1891	Dr JOHN LEWIS	1965-1976
Dr MONCURE D CONWAY	1892-1897	LORD SORENSEN	1965-1971
		LORD BROCKWAY	1969-1988
APPOINTED LECTURERS		T F EVANS	1972-2008
HERBERT BURROWS	1907-1922	PETER CRONIN	1972-1978
JOHN A HOBSON	1907-1940	HECTOR HAWTON	1974-1975
Rt Hon J M ROBERTSON	1907-1933	W H LIDDELL	1977-1983
JOSEPH McCABE	1907-1955	NICOLAS WALTER	1978-2000
S K RATCLIFFE	1915-1958	Dr HARRY STOPES-ROE	1978-2014
Dr C DELISLE BURNS	1918-1942	BARBARA SMOKER	1989-

SOUTH PLACE ETHICAL SOCIETY HAS DEVELOPED FROM A RELIGIOUS GROUP ALLIED TO THE BAPTISTS WHO ESTABLISHED THEMSELVES IN BISHOPSGATE IN 1793. THIS CONGREGATION WHICH LATER BECAME UNITARIAN BUILT THE CHAPEL IN SOUTH PLACE FINSBURY IN 1823 DURING THE MINISTRIES OF WILLIAM JOHNSON FOX AND OF MONCURE D CONWAY IT BECAME WELL KNOWN AS A HOME OF PROGRESSIVE RELIGIOUS THOUGHT AND IN 1888 ADOPTED THE NAME OF SOUTH PLACE ETHICAL SOCIETY. SINCE 1897 THERE HAS BEEN A ROTA OF APPOINTED LECTURERS INSTEAD OF A MINISTER. THE CONWAY HALL PREMISES WERE ERECTED BY THE SOCIETY AND OCCUPIED IN 1929. THE WORDS SOUTH PLACE ARE RETAINED IN THE SOCIETY'S NAME IN MEMORY OF THE FAMOUS OLD CHAPEL.

The Ethical Society's memorial board

the years in Conway Hall was with the palaeontologist Kenneth Oakley, who made a name for himself in 1953 by having the skull of the supposed 'missing link', Piltdown Man, radio-carbon-dated, thus proving that it was a forgery. He helped me write an article about it, rather like a detective story, and we became close friends.

As for Piltdown, I have never accepted the common assumption that Charles Dawson was the 1913 hoaxer – my number-one suspect always being the Modernist Jesuit priest and theologian Teilhard de Chardin. It was he who pounced on the clinching brown-stained tooth in the brown East Sussex gravel. He also had the vital motivation, as a keen evolutionist, of wanting the Vatican to accept natural selection and the descent of man. In his more mature years he always clammed up when Piltdown was mentioned.

UNHOLY WOMAN

The humanist psychologist Margaret Knight, who, being a few years my senior, was ahead of me in having read and thought her way out of Christianity, had for some years been badgering the BBC to give her radio access on the Home Service (now Radio 4) for a talk refuting the view that moral education must be based on supernatural sanctions. Though the Home Service was less progressive than the BBC's Third Programme, she was finally invited to Broadcasting House in 1954 to discuss her proposal, and it was decided that she could give two prime-time talks, which would include advice to fellow non-believers as to what they might honestly tell their children about religion.

To listen to her first talk, scheduled for the evening of 5th January 1955, I remember secretly switching on the radio in the kitchen while the rest of the family were sitting around the fire in the living-room.

The talk, though thoughtful, was diplomatic. But it caused a newspaper uproar. 'Peterborough' in the *Daily Telegraph* called upon God and the BBC to ban the second broadcast. But that was nothing to the *Sunday Graphic*'s front-page headline on 9th January. In two-inch letters it read 'THE UNHOLY Mrs KNIGHT', with a photograph of a staid middle-aged woman – 'in place of the usually rather different feminine portraits', to quote Kingsley Martin in the *New Statesman*. Fortunately, burning female apostates at the stake was no longer legal.

In future years, Margaret Knight became a friend of mine, though we were generally separated by the distance between London and Aberdeen.

CHAPTER FIVE
BUSINESS OF LIFE

THE COURSE that I took in Pitman's shorthand in 1946 is something I have never regretted. In fact, I think that phonetic shorthand, or else a half-speed phonetic writing system (such as Bernard Shaw advocated), should be taught in secondary schools, as a core subject.

Not only did shorthand-typing keep me from penury over the years – 'temping' whenever I ran out of money and credit – but I still use it for my personal notes. Moreover, I was to become known as the world's foremost transcriber of Bernard Shaw's shorthand drafts, for which I received remuneration from manuscript dealers and collectors, museums, scholars, writers and so on.

EMPLOYMENT

The occasional temporary jobs I took, which were always available through the temping agencies, included some really interesting assignments. One was as personal secretary to Brigadier Young, author of the best-seller *Rommel*, in the months leading up to its publication. In the office of Collins, his publishers, I bullied Princess Margaret's then boyfriend, who was working there, to get the misprints corrected, and dealt with some other important people. I also worked on the serialisation of *Rommel* for a Sunday newspaper, and when Rommel's son, Manfred, came across his father's copiously annotated copy of Lord Wavell's *Generals and Generalship*, I got permission to send it to Wavell, shortly before his death.

Another interesting job was in a small quirky firm in Fitzrovia, owned and run by a Frenchman, Guy Rouilly. Rather euphemistically, he called himself a medical supplier; in fact, he was a human osteologist – meaning, to use an irresistible pun, that the backbone of his business was the sale of human skeletons; his firm being the last in Europe to stock them. Rival firms were now selling plastic skeletons, and I can hear in my mind's ear Rouilly's scathing dismissal of them: 'Toys! Nothing but toys!'.

Our customers were mainly medical students, who needed a 'half-set' – that is, an articulated skeleton minus one arm and one leg. Though students were tending to opt now for the cheaper plastic skeletons, any who bought the real thing were able to sell it back to us for re-sale at the end of their tuition period. Masonic lodges were also good customers, their orders comprising a skull and pair of femurs (for the time-honoured skull and crossbones), while a skull that actually boasted 32 teeth would demand a higher price as a 'dental skull', usually bought by dentists. Skulls were also bought, or hired, by theatres and television producers putting on *Hamlet*, while articulated skeletons were required for museums and other exhibitions.

One of the young men employed in the firm had the job

of articulating the skeletons, by drilling holes in the bones and threading them on to wire or the more expensive catgut. He was snapped up for the television panel game *What's My Line?*, and unsurprisingly the panel failed to guess the answer.

The skeletons mostly came from India, where impoverished families would accept a small sum for the corpses of their family members, meaning that they also saved the cost of a funeral. The bones were separated from the flesh in a factory in Calcutta, then crated up for shipment to our office.

If there was too much grease left in them, they had to be boiled and hung up to dry, and some of my friends, calling for me there, were really scared of the skeletons hanging from the ceiling. I myself could never see anything scary in dead bones, which have no consciousness, whereas I would have been too squeamish to work, for instance, in a veterinary surgeon's with suffering animals, let alone an abattoir.

Before my time, Mr Rouilly had purchased a consignment of larger, younger, superior skeletons, but now had none left, and he was always ready to buy any back for more than he had received for them. 'Beautiful skeletons!' he used to sigh. They had come from Soviet Russia, and he got me to write once or twice to the Russian suppliers to enquire whether there were any more available. I was not sorry that we never received a reply, as I was sure their availability relied on political state executions.

I enjoyed having long, time-wasting discussions with Mr Rouilly on religion and philosophy, and remember the

French intonation of his exclamatory 'I am a *bad* Catholic – but you are a *terrible* Catholic!'

His permanent secretary, whose place I had taken while she was in hospital, came back – only to give in her notice. Rouilly then invited me to stay on permanently in her stead, and as I quite liked the working set-up and its flexibility, I accepted.

During one of his nostalgic visits to France, that country was paralysed by a general strike, depriving it of postal and telephone services and any possibility of international travel, so Rouilly was unable to give any orders to his work force. Knowing how to deal with new orders, I did so in his enforced absence, and on his return, pleasantly surprised by this, he paid me a good bonus.

However, when he decided to appoint a manager, so that he could retire (he was already well past retirement age), he did not consider offering me the position, since managers obviously had to be men. A male manager was duly engaged, and Rouilly actually asked me to show the man the ropes. Much to his mystification, I handed in my notice.

By this time I was in my thirties and decided it was a good age to retire finally from full-time permanent employment. For one thing, I had come to realise that going out to work costs employees a sizable portion of the money earned. Increasing rail and bus fares raise the cost of commuting to the place of work, especially if in central London; alternatively, the shorter the journey the more costly the accommodation. Employees also have to spend money on decent clothes to wear to work, instead of slopping around all day in a dressing-gown, and to eat expensive meals out instead of cheaply at home. Not to mention such statutory plunder as income tax and national insurance contributions.

So I never took another permanent full-time job – only temping and intermittent freelance money-earners with flexible hours. I did, however, for the sake of the distant state pension, always buy weekly N. I. stamps to stick on my contributions card, since the rate for a non-employed (not unemployed) woman was very much lower than that for a man. (It was one of the few advantages of being female.)

Passport identity, 1958

HOUSING

In the mid-1950s my parents were planning to retire to rural Sussex, while I had no wish to leave London. I therefore needed to find somewhere else to live, within my limited budget; limited because of my retirement at the age of 30-odd from regular paid employment in favour of spending my time in the reading-room of the British Museum – as Bernard Shaw had done seven decades earlier.

A friend of my mother's from church told me that she knew an elderly widow in a down-market area of Forest Hill, Dalmain Road, who was looking for a tenant for the top two rooms of her house – a three-storey Victorian low-ceilinged terraced cottage, which had been bought originally by her late husband, probably for no more than the cost of a posh restaurant meal today.

The house contained no such luxuries as an indoor lavatory, central heating or hot water. But I was not bothered about that. At least it had running drinkable water. So I arranged to visit the landlady, a Mrs Birch, and was pleased that my mother agreed to accompany me.

I feared that I might be quizzed about religion, but the only stipulation Mrs Birch made was that I should not hang clothes out on a Sunday! 'Oh no,' interposed my mother; 'Barbara would never do that.'

Rent for the two rooms was calculated to meet the cost of the local rates (council tax) on the house – only twelve shillings and sixpence (in decimal currency, 62.5 pence) per week. It was also necessary to keep a shilling piece on hand for the gas-meter.

I lived there for nine years, and would never have left had not the Greater London Council (then a housing authority) aspired to colonise several streets for an extensive 1960s-style property development. Instead of simply modifying the existing houses or replacing them terrace by terrace, the councillors planned to buy up umpteen acres for wholesale demolition before embarking on any rebuilding.

Many of the houses were rented through agents, making it difficult to trace some of the freeholders; so it was years before the total area was owned by the GLC. Meanwhile, dozens of the properties they did own were vacated and 'tinned-up', while homelessness prevailed. One elderly couple I remember crying because they had been left as isolated tenants in a sea of empty properties, with rats facing them whenever they used the outside lavatory. And I saw vacant houses in our road being up-graded – not for occupation but so that their remote owners could obtain higher prices for them from the GLC. It was a real-life echo of Shaw's first play, *Widowers' Houses*.

The situation raised my missionary hackles, and I began a hostile correspondence with the chairman of the GLC housing committee. He was an upper-crust Tory, but fair-minded, and eventually he offered to come and inspect some of the houses that I said had been left empty after modernisation. He brought along a workman whom I dubbed an official burglar, his job being to break into any of the tinned-up houses that I stipulated. There was one house I particularly had my eye on, having witnessed its refurbishment to a high-grade finish, since when it had never been occupied. As we went in, the GLC councillor commented 'I wouldn't mind living in this one myself.' Later he relinquished his chairmanship of the GLC housing committee and founded a community housing association, Quadrant – for which he privately gave me credit.

Mrs Birch, being incontestably the freehold owner of our house, was approached by an official early on, and advised to evict me so that she could sell the vacant house to the GLC – which, it was promised, would then allot her a nice modern flat elsewhere.

Ascertaining that I had lived in the house long enough to have statutory security of tenure, I eventually obtained an apology from the GLC. But they had, of course, whetted my landlady's appetite, so I felt I had to vacate the flat.

LESLIE

By that time I was fortunate enough to have a well-heeled humanist life-partner, Leslie Johnson, and as I wanted to move he bought me an early Victorian house (partly tenanted and therefore not too expensive) in Stanstead Grove – an unmade road in Catford. It was one of the oldest houses in south-east London, but pre-war it had acquired running water and a back extension containing two bathrooms. The ground floor being already let, I then let the semi-basement and lived on the top floor myself. And there I will stay until chapter 9.

Since the house had only one door-bell, I stuck a notice beside it giving my name for a single ring and the other oc-cupants' names for double or treble rings respectively. One

Sunday, when I was the only person at home, there was a double ring, which I ignored, then a treble ring. I decided to open the door, and was confronted by two missionary Jehovah's Witnesses. 'Oh!' exclaimed one, 'we didn't ring for you; we know you are an enemy of the Lord!'

I met Leslie first in a television green-room shortly after the introduction of commercial TV channels. We were both competitors in a prize quiz programme – a sort of forerunner of *Mastermind*, as one chose one's own specialist subject. Mine was Bernard Shaw; Leslie's Gilbert and Sullivan. We had a chat, and found we shared an addiction to literary competitions, but we did not exchange names.

Leslie was the joint owner-occupier with his sister Joyce of a vintage house in Tunbridge Wells, and on returning home he told her about me. She too was keen on literary competitions, and she guessed from my dual interest in them and in Bernard Shaw that I must be Barbara Smoker. The following week Leslie and I met again on the quiz programme, and that was the beginning of our close relationship.

He was thirty years my senior – in fact, the same age as my father – but the age gap between us never bothered me. Like Dad, he had experienced the horror of trench warfare, and it made him a staunch lifelong pacifist. We also shared other radical liberal views, including atheistic humanism. Though I did not share his religion of five-day cricket, with special devotion to the Kent county team, I was blessed by being related to Saint Frank Woolley.

For the first year or two of our partnership, Leslie was

still a civil servant in the Estate Duty Office. He then retired
– with a good pension.

He was a pastmaster of cryptic crosswords, having solved
them and compiled them since the day they were invented
under the original name 'acrostics'. On Sundays we often
visited friends in Hampstead who would buy two copies of
the *Observer* so as to hold a speed competition in completing
the Ximenes puzzle, between Leslie on one side and the other
three or four of us on the other, and our multiple brains
hardly ever beat his one.

He taught me the art of compiling cryptic crosswords. In
those days they featured in both the *Radio Times* and *Kenya
Radio Times*, with specialist radio and television references
in the clues and solutions, and Leslie often compiled them
for both papers. He then shared the job with me, and after
his death I continued doing them until the papers stopped
using crosswords. I also contributed clues for the one in the
Manchester Guardian.

In the Shaw Society's journal, *The Shavian,* I introduced a
prize crossword containing Shavian references, but the same
few people kept winning the prize, so I had to drop it. Nowadays the only crossword I compile is one containing local
place names for the *Lewisham Pensioners' Gazette*, the solution
appearing in the same issue.

During the twelve years we had together, until his death
in 1969, Leslie spent half of each week with his sister and
the other half in my primitive flat or, later, the house he
had bought for me. That pattern, rather than the more
conventional monotony of day-to-day cohabiting, I would

recommend universally for the durability of living relationships. I always looked forward to his weekly arrival, and we would plan events for the next three or four days, rather like a holiday. As for actual holidays, we enjoyed a week on a literary package tour of Dublin and also a SAGA Mediterranean cruise with its presentations by leading classicists.

On the days we were apart, Leslie always wrote me a long witty and loving letter – physically long, as he usually wrote on the lengthy galley-paper used for journals. (In those days a letter posted in Kent in time for the evening collection was reliably delivered to its London addressee early next morning. There was no such thing as first-class post.)

IQ

At that time the society Mensa – founded in the mid-1950s with the aim of bringing together people of high intelligence from every sphere of expertise – demanded of its membership an IQ above that of the top 0.5 percent (half of one percent) of the general population. Leslie was interested in it, and applied in both our names for membership. After passing the initial test, we were each called to the London School of Economics for an extensive psychologist-supervised written examination. This incorporated a speed-test by dint of including far more problems that anyone could possibly solve in the hour available. I therefore decided to concentrate on my strongest territory – language-based questions – rather than take up time puzzling over mathematical brain-teasers. Those I left to the end, then merely guessed feasible answers to most of them.

I was informed that on the Binet scale my IQ came to 156, at the level of genius. Moreover, I was told that this was almost unheard-of in a woman. (Apparently, both geniuses and morons are almost exclusively male; women generally cluster near the centre of the IQ spectrum.) I was well aware that my real degree of intelligence was flattered by the score of 156 – though perhaps my recourse to guesswork was itself an intelligent move.

Leslie failed to make the grade, but no allowance had been made for age – as it should have been – and of course he did not sink to the strategy of guesswork.

He insisted on paying for my Mensa enrolment. However, horrified to see that the society's journal contained readers' letters indicating belief in Christ's bodily resurrection, I refused to renew my membership for the following year.

Some years later, to augment the society's membership, its benchmark for admission was lowered to the supposed IQ of the general top two percent.

CND

Every Easter weekend we went on the four-day Aldermaston ban-the-bomb march, organised by the Campaign for Nuclear Disarmament (CND). There were always varied religious groups marching with their sectarian banners, though most of them represented no more than a small minority of the religion's membership; so I decided that humanism should likewise show its face, even if some members of the humanist movement did not agree with unilateral nuclear

Leslie, *en route* to an Easter CND march and rally

disarmament. I therefore made my own canvas banner, proclaiming HUMANISTS ARE MARCHING.

Although by that time I was more involved in 'direct action' (also known as 'civil disobedience') than with the law-abiding CND, I still collected subscriptions for them. One year I also organised local hired buses to transport marchers from Catford to the day's starting point each morning of the Easter march.

In (I think) 1961, the National Secular Society began taking part in the annual march, and, as colleagues, with some dozen humanists marching behind my banner, I took up the position immediately ahead of the NSS banner. One of the official CND photographs was a good one of both contingents, so I obtained a copy of it which I gave to the then editor of *The Humanist*, Hector Hawton, and he used it on the front-cover of his next issue. He told me afterwards that some readers complained strongly about this plug for unilateral nuclear disarmament. More than half-a-century later, a small reproduction of the same photograph was included in the history published by the NSS to commemorate the 150th anniversary of its foundation in 1866. In the photo I am holding one pole of my banner, with Leslie walking just behind it.

Easter Monday 1962, with my home-made banner

Coming across a new American slogan, 'Make Love Not War', which I rather liked, I suggested to some of our own medal vendors that they purloin it, but no-one was willing to spend money on it. I therefore did so myself, with an order to a firm of medal makers. Selling the medals on the march, I made a small profit from them. The following year, however, I wondered whether the slogan had been taken too literally – as there seemed to be quite a baby boom among the young generation of marchers.

ETHICAL RECORD

One thing I was always good at, and therefore enjoyed, was finding the best words to express ideas in writing, and this, combined with being a born fault-finder, made me a natural editor. In fact, in my last year or two at school, the English mistress entrusted me with editing the school magazine.

Some fifteen years later, Bernard Shaw's wit having prompted me (in his own lifetime) to join the Shaw Society, I became editor of its journal, *The Shavian*. This led to my being invited in 1964 to edit the South Place Ethical Society's journal, which mainly comprised a record of the summarised lectures; at the time retaining its original title, *The Monthly Record*. I lost no time in changing the title to *The Ethical Record*, which is its title to this day; and I remained its editor for six years – until getting the sack.

The Society, having been founded in the 18th century as a dissident Christian congregation, initially in opposition to the heinous espousal of eternal punishment, had always enjoyed charity status under the historical category of religion; and Conway Hall officially remained a place of religious worship.

As such, it was authorised to hold legal weddings, two of the Society's senior members being accredited registrars. One of the two at that time was the then General Secretary, Peter Cadogan – who would now be designated Chief Executive Officer – and (rather conceitedly) he got a Sunday newspaper colour-supplement to feature the Conway Hall weddings. It thus came to the attention of the Charity Commission that the Society retained the privileges of its historical religious category, though no longer actually religious in doctrine or practice, so we lost the financial benefits of charity status, not to mention the right to register marriages.

While I had admired Peter's inventive leadership in anti-war direct action some fifteen years earlier, I was sorry to find now that in the SPES context he was on the 'spiritual' (though not theistic) side. It was probably at his instigation that a caucus of long-standing members of the Society conspired to re-introduce minor religious practices into the Society's activities in order to regain its valuable charity status. This conspiracy was leaked to me by an old member, Edwina Palmer, who told me which members were involved, gave me the name of the hotel where their secret meetings were held (to avoid using our own premises), and also the dates of all their meetings.

Deciding to use my editorial prerogative for clandestine whistle-blowing, I wrote it all up as a five-page editorial, to be substituted for the usual single-page editorial in the July 1970 issue of the *ER*, then showed it to Harold Blackham

THE ETHICAL RECORD
(Formerly 'The Monthly Record')

Vol. 75, No. 7   JULY/AUGUST 1970

The views expressed in this journal are not necessarily those of the Society

EDITORIAL

Elections — for Parliament and South Place

THE nation has recently been subjected to an orgy of electioneering, entailing mutual childish abuse of personalities, appeals to the electorate on a most selfish level, and contradictory prophecies by statistical soothsayers. It may not all have been clean fighting, but at least everyone knew there was a fight on. It was generally known to be a struggle for power between two major opposing factions, called Parties, each allowed by the rules of the game to canvass for support — within certain prescribed limits of expenditure and abuse.

Suppose, however, that there were no explicit acknowledgment that separate Parties existed, and there was no provision for canvassing, yet one faction (a minority), sinking all its internal differences, held secret meetings and carried out selective canvassing, while everyone else remained not only unorganised but, for the most part, unaware that the political game was being played at all, let alone that coalition and canvassing were apparently allowed by the unwritten rules. Such a situation would smack more of conspiracy for a *coup d'état* than of democratic procedure. Yet this is actually a description of what has been happening, on a much smaller scale, in our own Society, our recent Annual General Meeting being analogous to the General Election.

After notice of resignation as General Secretary had been given by Mr. H. G. Knight last November, invitations were received by selected members of the Society to attend a private meeting at the Whitehall Hotel on December 16 — "with", to quote the invitation (signed by B. O. Warwick, C. E. Barralet, J. W. Blundell, L. L. Booker, and V. G. Howlett) "the knowledge and agreement of our Secretary, Mr. Knight". Some of those who attended that meeting, alienated by the proceedings, have informed us that a motion (proposed by Miss G. Hawtin) that a dossier should be built up on the Society's Registrar was actually put to the vote; and derogatory insinuations were made also about other uninvited members. A second clandestine meeting took place the following month. A third, arranged for April 6, was cancelled, but further (though smaller) meetings of the faction have apparently taken place subsequently, in spite of assurances made to the Society's General Committee by one of the above signatories that the meetings had been discontinued and that a previous decision of the General Committee to invite members of the faction to a joint meeting for the discussion of any grievances was no longer appropriate.

Meanwhile, Mr. Peter Cadogan had been appointed General Secre-

3

My swan-song as editor of *The Ethical Record*

for his approval. This he gave, with only one reservation: 'As long as you don't mind getting the sack.' I deemed the whistle well worth the sack. As the Society had historically rebelled against Christian dogmatics, my editorial was really a rebellion within a rebellion.

Peter Cadogan always received from the printers an advance vetting copy of the *ER* before they distributed the members' copies individually by mail, so I told the head of the printing firm that on this occasion he should delay sending Peter his advance copy until all the members' copies were in the post. On publication day, the printer telephoned me to say he had just had an agitated phone call from Peter Cadogan, telling him not to send out the members' copies

Brandishing hat and shoes ahead of SPES group ramble, c. 1970

114

of the journal. 'So I had to tell him', the printer said, 'that unfortunately they were already in the post'.

A SPES Special General Committee meeting was then called to consider the future of the insubordinate editor, and of course I attended it. After the indictment, Rose Bush, who was in the chair, turned to me: 'Miss Smoker, I must ask for your resignation as editor.' 'I have no intention of resigning', I replied. 'If you want to get rid of me, you will have to kick me out.' So they did.

CHARITABLE

The Society having lost the benefits of charity status, the membership voted to lodge a legal appeal to regain it – but not to go down the route of pretending to be a religion.

We were summoned in 1980 to the Royal Courts of Justice for the appeal hearing, where Peter Cadogan was to speak as our principal witness. The prior members' meeting admonished him to steer clear of the religious gambit, but in the event he contravened this instruction. Ludicrously, he even claimed in court that the convivial distribution of coffee and biscuits at the end of our lecture meetings was a sort of Holy Communion!

However, we were very fortunate with the particular judge assigned to us – Mr Justice Dillon. While he refused to concede that SPES could still be considered a religious body, he decided it merited charity status under two other categories: Education and Public Benefit. This was the best possible outcome of the case for us; but the extortionate lawyers' fees for the appeal left the Society heavily in debt for a year or more – even depending on loans and donations to pay the electricity bills for Conway Hall. The British Humanist Association then obtained charity status on the SPES coat-tails, at no cost to them.

GAMBLING

The legalisation of betting-shops in 1961 put an end to the absurd situation whereby the upper classes were allowed to gamble on credit while working-class cash betting was illegal, with street bookmakers employing look-outs for police constables on the beat.

At first it was against the law for the new betting-shops to contain seats, which would encourage gamblers to 'loiter', wasting their time and money. But such restrictions soon went by the board, and nowadays the shops are furnished comfortably – in fact, made perhaps too attractive, even to the provision of free refreshments for lingerers, so that the shops become second homes for many compulsive gamblers.

In the mid-1960s I had a fairly modest weekly credit account by telephone with Tote Investors, and one week early in 1966 I finished up owing them £43. It was hardly a fortune, but, being a bit short of ready money, I decided to postpone paying them till the following week. A few days later, however, I received a letter from the Tote threatening to take me to court for my failure to pay the debt. This surprised me, not only because of the comparatively small sum involved and the meagre time allowed for paying it, but because I thought that simply pleading the Gaming Acts would be a good defence in court.

The 19th-century Gaming Acts established that debts incurred by way of 'gaming' were irrecoverable at law – mainly to safeguard land-owning gamblers from losing their estates and rendering themselves and their families destitute. And these redemptive laws were still on the statute book. So, thinking the Tote people must be bluffing, I decided to withhold payment of the £43, just to see what would happen.

After my move from Dalmain Road to Stanstead Grove, Tote Investors sent two legal representatives to serve a prosecution writ on me complaining that it had been difficult and time-wasting for them to locate me as they only had my old address. I decided to ignore the writ, mainly because Leslie, agreeing that I was obviously covered by the Gaming Acts, offered to back me by meeting any litigation costs I might incur.

In due course I was summoned to the Royal Courts of Justice, and took a good deal of trouble preparing my case with reference to the legal precedents. Surprisingly, the three judges assigned to this minor lawsuit were three of the most senior law lords, including Master of the Rolls Lord Denning – presumably because of the huge sum that the Tote stood to lose if the judgment were to go against them. And the press, interested as always in a David-Goliath story, took it up in a big way.

When the case adjourned for lunch I went out into Carey Street, carrying my briefcase. Seeing a press photographer on my trail, I began walking purposefully (as my Trincomalee friend Pauline had taught me), and the photograph of me that appeared in the tabloids next morning made me look quite formidable.

However, that did not win me the case. The judges found against me, on the grounds that 'gaming' means both sides must be able to win or lose. Since the Tote, unlike a bookmaker, pays out only the amount of money covenanted to the pool on the event, the judgment was that it cannot lose, so is not gaming, and is therefore not subject to the Gaming Acts.

After delivering the judgment, Lord Denning congratulated me on my 'elegant' defence and asked me how I knew so much about the relevant preceding cases. Probably thinking that I had employed solicitors for the research, he looked astonished when I replied that I had merely looked up law-books that I found in the reading-room of the British Museum. The three judges then gave me express permission to appeal to the House of Lords.

It had been mentioned during the case that I was the editor of a journal called *The Ethical Record*, and I was worried about this appearing in the newspapers, possibly with some ribald comment, since such publicity would hardly go down well with the South Place Ethical Society's General Committee. Therefore, surrounded and questioned by a dozen journalists as I left the court, I said I only hoped that the word 'Ethical' would not appear anywhere; and one of the journalists asked all the others to agree to that preclusion. They did so, and every newspaper kept to that promise, with just one exception – *The Daily Telegraph* – whose news report did in fact cause some hostile reaction from one or two members of SPES.

Were I to appeal to the House of Lords, I reasoned, I might possibly have the same three law-lords again, but they could well come to the opposite decision, since my argument this time round would concentrate on the grounds they had given for their original judgment – grounds that I had not foreseen in my presentation. I would be able to point out that, since the bookmakers' starting-price is based on the total of all other bets laid, their SP and the Tote dividend are always close. Only in the case of fixed odds and early prices might they differ, and there the bookies were more, not less, likely to be at a greater risk than the Tote. So it was unfair that, unlike the Tote, they were deemed to be engaged in gaming and therefore subject to the Gaming Acts – making them vulnerable to defaulting punters. Also, ironically, the Tote shortly afterwards actually made large losses through their profits being insufficient to cover the administrative costs.

Moreover, the Gaming Acts were obviously intended to protect the gambler from himself; it was therefore hardly relevant whether or not the recipients of his wagers were themselves at risk. Besides, they too were covered by the Acts, so could not be sued by punters for their winnings – though any professional bookmakers who defaulted would, of course, soon be out of business.

The Tote directors were obviously uneasy about my going to appeal, for they bribed me not to do so, by letting me off the considerable costs as well as the negligible original debt. But my main reason for deciding not to proceed to the

Challenging the Tote

proffered appeal was that Leslie was reluctant to underwrite it, since it could bankrupt him were I to lose again.

Having lost the case, I quickly dropped out of the news. Had I won – resulting in losses to the Tote amounting to many millions of pounds – I would have been eminently news-worthy. Incidentally, some years later one of my nephews, who was a law student, told me that my case was the subject of a footnote in a textbook on the law of contract.

The level playing field I had tried to establish on behalf of bookmakers (as well as Tote punters), in relation to Tote Investors, was eventually brought about by the electronic revolution, which, facilitating the instantaneous transfer of stake money, rendered credit betting practically extinct.

FEMINISM

The 1960s decade, though so deplorable for social housing in Britain, was superlative in other spheres of legislation, being the decade that saw capital punishment abolished, homosexuality decriminalised and safe abortion made available.

It was in 1968, after arduous campaigning, that abortion was finally legalised in Britain. I had been writing insistently that women must have the right of jurisdiction over their own bodies, including the right to terminate a pregnancy – at least before the foetus is viable, and, indeed, even up to term in serious cases of foetal abnormality. To this day, there is one country of the UK, Northern Ireland, which outlaws all abortion as a criminal offence, on religious grounds.

There was continued opposition from fundamentalist Christians everywhere to all of the humanitarian reforms, and in 1974 I decided to make the still contentious issue of abortion the subject of my presidential address to the NSS AGM. If, I maintained, a supreme creator existed, he would have to be the greatest abortionist of all, since the incidence of spontaneous abortion far exceeds that of induced termination. My peroration, therefore, was a prayer for use by the 'pro-life' lobby: 'O, thou great abortionist! Thine is the monopoly of righteous abortion, for ever and ever. Amen!'

MORALITY

'If you don't believe in God or a future life, what's to prevent you from committing murder or any other crime?' The implication of this question is that those asking it would themselves enjoy committing atrocious crimes if not prevented by fear of Hell.

Yet the question was often asked of Darwinists in the nineteenth century, as a widespread reaction to natural selection – which side-lined creation. Though it was asked less frequently in the twentieth century, I was still often asked it when on radio and TV programmes with audience participation, and it is sometimes heard even today – despite the fact that atheists, in their increasing numbers, are no worse transgressors than believers. In fact, though the supposed godless crimes are likely to incur judicial imprisonment, statistics show consistently that non-believers are well underrepresented among convicted prisoners – which can only mean that they are either more law-abiding or cleverer in escaping the law than believers are.

However, there is an underlying theological reason

that may well account for greater immorality among god-believers: the doctrine that worship of God, and obedience to his revealed demands, must come first – human welfare only second. Yet the sole rationally defensible basis for morality is promotion of the welfare of human beings, followed by that of other sentient animals with which we share the planet. This is the evolutionary basis of morality. Biologically inherited, some kind of morality is common to every living species, as part of its proved fitness to survive. The long-term welfare of the planet itself is also widely recognised now as an important element of human morality, for the sake of future generations.

But what sin do theists inveigh against more than any other? Simply disobedience, and the scepticism that leads to disobedience. Not cruelty, not failure to work out the probable consequences of any action – just disobedience against the supposed deity and its purported revelation. Indeed, religions of the book ascribe all of the ills of the world to 'man's first disobedience' at the woman's instigation in the Garden of Eden.

The pathological condition of Obsessive Compulsive Disorder (OCD) is the agreed diagnosis for those who feel they have to keep performing certain rituals in order to avoid some illogical misfortune – and the irrational behaviour is similar when people who belong to a particular religion assiduously practise its prescribed rituals, including repetitious prayer. Perhaps, therefore, we could start using the term 'religious OCD' as a telling synonym for pious fundamentalism.

CHAPTER SIX
SEDITION

WHILE the law-abiding Campaign for Nuclear Disarmament became a mass movement in the early 1960s, attracting large numbers to its Aldermaston marches each Easter, those carrying out illegal direct action against nuclear arms naturally remained comparatively small, since few supporters were willing to go so far as to risk imprisonment. In 1960 Bertrand Russell therefore founded the Committee of 100 (C100), based on the idea that if 100 members were equally guilty of planning acts of civil disobedience it would be difficult for the authorities to put them all on trial together and sentence them all to long prison sentences, so there would be safety in numbers.

DIRECT ACTION

However, Russell's scheme failed, the government being less concerned with justice than he had imagined. Faced with a large illegal demonstration at the American air-force base at Wethersfield, Essex, with 850 arrests, the Crown Prosecution Office simply picked six relatively unknown people among the organisers to be charged – representing the lot. The five men and one woman, dubbed 'the Wethersfield Six', were then convicted and sentenced to imprisonment for eighteen months and one year respectively. The woman, Helen Allegranza, who had merely taken the role of welfare officer for the demonstrators, was kept on prescribed tranquilisers while in Holloway Prison, and after release she committed suicide.

As for the men, two of them, Pat Pottle and Michael Randle, together with an Irish escapee Sean Bourke, plotted and engineered the amazingly successful escape (to Russia) of fellow prisoner double-agent George Blake – who, convicted of betraying other British agents to the Russian equivalent of MI6, was serving an excessive 42 years' imprisonment for that felony. And the springers were never apprehended. By the time they went public about it, years later, it would have looked ridiculous to put them on trial. After Pat Pottle's death, at the age of 62, I attended his memorial meeting, where one of George Blake's three sons made a surprise appearance, in gratitude for the decades of freedom his father had been given.

Following the celebrated Wethersfield demonstration, I volunteered to work in the office of the C100's London wing, on preparations for a public assembly in Trafalgar Square banned by the police. A press photographer paid us a visit, and in the large photograph that appeared in the *Daily Telegraph* of 15th September 1961, there I am (unnamed but recognisable), crawling on the floor, parcelling up posters. It was the daily newspaper that my parents took, and, seeing it, Mum phoned me early that morning to warn me that if I got into trouble I should not expect any help from the family. But I knew that her bark, however gentle, was worse than her bite.

The Trafalgar Square assembly, which became a sit-down, was very successful, with 12,000 committed demonstrators taking part. It was then mooted that we might attract an even larger number on the next demo if we were to offer the reassurance of prior pledges of participation, making the intended safety in numbers less assailable. We decided to do so, together with an undertaking to cancel the assembly if we received fewer than 7,000 pledges for it.

I had already been convicted for my part in several illegal demonstrations, and for one of them still owed a fine, which I was refusing to pay, thereby inviting imprisonment, and this outcome happened to catch up with me while I was helping to collect the pledges. About to be arrested, I phoned the C100 office to say I would not be available for a couple of weeks – only to be told they could not afford to let me go at that point and would rather I paid the fine. Therefore, when two policemen arrived at my flat to escort me to jail, I handed them the cash for the fine – much to their annoyance.

Sadly, we had been too optimistic in expecting more than 7,000 pledges for the second Trafalgar Square sit-down, and in the event they fell a bit short of the stipulated number. It was argued, however, that rather than cancel the demonstration we could still go ahead with it provided we announced that all the pledges we had received were annulled. However, Bertrand Russell protested that this was not what we had said, and we must keep to the cancellation of the demo, as promised. Most of us thought our alternative solution was good enough, but he then came to London to attend our next meeting, threatening to resign his C100 membership unless we cancelled the sit-down. So we had no option but to do so – and this negative outcome spelt the decline and dissolution of the whole organisation.

I still think that Russell was unnecessarily scrupulous. On the other hand, he had heroically, in his 90th year, spent a fortnight in jail – a repeat performance of his imprisonment almost half-a-century earlier because, like Socrates, he was defying the establishment and 'corrupting the young'. During his trial I stood in a group of supporters, holding a CND 'lollipop', and held it up behind his head when he emerged from the court. In the photograph that appeared in the *Guardian*, it looked like a halo!

SPIES FOR PEACE

Prior to leaving home on Easter Saturday 1963 for the starting point of the second day of the annual Aldermaston march, I was busy preparing a picnic lunch for Leslie and myself when the postman came with a batch of letters, and I asked Leslie to open them.

Slitting open a rather fat manilla envelope, he suddenly exclaimed 'Hey! This is really something!'

Emanating from a clandestine group calling itself 'Spies for Peace', it was a document of several 'foolscap' pages, duplicated from typewritten stencils – the precursors of photocopies – and it described, with illustrations, the 'Regional Seat of Government No. 6' (RSG6). This appeared to be a secret government bolt-hole, similar to Hitler's bunker in

Berlin 18 years earlier, but now brought up-to-date and sealed against nuclear radiation. In response to the government's fear of a nuclear attack – not from Germany now but from Russia – it was earmarked as a protective refuge, exclusively for VIPs and military personnel.

Well-equipped and furnished, it was in complete readiness for occupation, but had to be kept strictly hush-hush lest ordinary members of the public fail to appreciate the need for its restricted purpose. One day, however, two young C100 supporters had by chance stumbled upon its unguarded grassy entrance. Naturally, they broke in. Finding it deserted and realising its significance, they made a detailed inventory of the contents, taking photographs. They then passed all the information on to leading activists of the C100, who, as Spies for Peace, proceeded to disseminate it – and to do so strategically.

It transpired that RSG6 was one of sixty such installations around the country. This one just happened to be located a few hundred yards off the route of the CND Easter march from Aldermaston to London – the perfect conveyance for the revelation of a state secret.

Hundreds of marchers had received the same item in their morning's postal delivery as I had, and thousands were soon apprised of it. Within hours, many were carrying banners giving the RSG6 location, chanting its name, and singing appropriate songs about secrets. At the lunch-time break, some, defying the chief CND organisers (who were desperately responsible to the police), turned off the prescribed route towards the hitherto secret bunker, and the

Defence of the Realm and Official Secrets Acts were power-less to stop them.

During the next few days, police carried out frenzied house and office searches, but to no avail. Like the Blake springers, the Spies for Peace had been too clever for them. Wearing gloves, they had left no finger-prints; the identical cheap paper and envelopes they used were available every-where and had been purchased over time in different chain stores; the mailing was carried out across a widespread area; and their stencilling typewriter, with other equipment, was already at the bottom of the Thames.

PROLIFERATION

Like medieval monks copying the Holy Bible, wide-spread cells of C100 supporters quickly stencilled innu-merable copies of the offending paper. The following Sunday morning I went out with a batch of them, calling on householders from door to door, like a Jehovah's Witness. 'Would you like to buy a government secret for sixpence?' I asked when they came to the door. Some of them were intrigued enough to hand me sixpence, but one of those who did so must have phoned the police as soon as I left. Suddenly the quiet residential street was invaded by police on motor-cycles.

Dropping my wares into my shopping-bag, I hurriedly crossed the road into a park, for an ostensible Sunday stroll, but soon felt a heavy hand on my shoulder. Its owner confiscated all my literature – including the CND's Black Paper, that was legal propaganda. A few weeks later I made an official complaint about the police theft of legal papers, whereupon they were returned to me – each one defaced in ink with the details of their seizure – though the copies of the incriminating document were never returned. But nor was I charged for any criminal offence.

Years later it transpired that the main executive of Spies for Peace was Nicolas Walter, who was also secretary of the Rationalist Press Association. He happily talked about the RSG6 exploit when it was too late to put him on trial. For minor acts of civil disobedience he did serve token prison sentences, and surprisingly said in fact he rather enjoyed the relaxing respite of those short holidays.

He was one of the most intelligent people I have ever known, though too much of a perfectionist to fulfil his true potential. In fact, his perfectionism was a trial to many of us, and I received my share of his obloquy over the years, but one day, on reading a letter of mine published in a leading paper, he phoned me with a memorable compliment: 'I wish I had written that'. Praise indeed!

Nicolas devoted his crusading life largely to the cause of freedom of information – not least of the opinions he opposed, provided only that there was an equal right of reply. Thus, when *Gay News* and its editor Denis Lemon were convicted of blasphemy (at the instigation of Mrs Mary Whitehouse) for the publication of a poem by James Kirkup, 'The love that Dares to Speak its Name', Nicolas – while loathing the poem's religiosity – devoted his time and energy to reproducing and distributing thousands of copies of it, under the imprint 'Free Speech Movement'. He thus vastly multiplied the number of readers from those of its original censored publication, but was never put on trial for it.

Sadly he died (of cancer) in 2000, aged 66. Strangely, the obituary article on him that appeared in *The Times* was printed alongside one he had written himself on a fellow campaigner.

EUROPEAN EXPEDITION

One of the most exciting C100 projects in which I participated was the motorcade expedition to Greece, in August 1963. The aim was to join an Aldermaston-style march in Athens against nuclear weapons, since the Greek citizens who did so were threatened with jail and the parliamentarian Deputy Gregori Lambrakis, who had planned the march, had been murdered by the Greek King's bodyguard – who was never prosecuted for it.

Some of our cars suffered breakdown on the way, and the rest were finally halted at the Austro-Jugoslavian border, where we mystified the border police with a politely limited sit-down protest. We were held at the frontier, free but immobile, for a week, and only two members of our hundred-strong expedition ever reached Athens, by hiding in a railway-train lavatory. I spent most of the week typing, on my lightweight typewriter, stencils of explanatory statements in English and my school German, printing them off and distributing them to tourists.

The return home was difficult, especially as, having no job to get home to, I had the lowest priority for a car seat. Finally, with only one day to spare before the expiry date of my passport, I was given a lift by two German pacifists to

On the Greek border, 1963 (I'm in the foreground wearing my CND headscarf)

a port in northern Germany for a boat home. Having several hours to wait there before the scheduled sailing, I was invited to the home of a young man for supper. His parents happened to be out, but I was welcomed by his octogenarian grandmother, whom I addressed in my scrappy German. To my amazement, she replied in perfect, though rather slow and stilted, English. 'Oh, you speak English!' I exclaimed. 'Yes', she replied, 'I spent a year in London when the old queen was on the throne' – and it transpired she had actually been presented as a debutante to Queen Victoria at the end of the 19th century.

GAMESMANSHIP

One of the Wethersfield Six was Terry Chandler, who, within six years of that baptism, stood in the Old Bailey dock for two more acts of civil disobedience, in 1963 and 1967. In the first indictment he was falsely charged with violence, and this was really serious, as all our demos were committed to non-violence. He therefore decided to subpoena at least a dozen 'character witnesses', of whom I was one, to vouch for his commitment to non-violence. The official subpoena summons that I received in the post was couched in 17th-century-style English, so that my first reaction was to suppose it was a practical joke. But it was no joke: it had the force of law, and there would be penalties for failing to answer it.

Hanging about for days from Tuesday, 3 December 1963, in the precincts of the court with all Terry's other witnesses, I wanted to take one day off for another engagement, so asked Terry the previous evening whether he would be calling me that day. He said he would not, so I took a chance and absented myself from the court. On my next arrival, a policeman accosted me with an accusation of truancy. 'You mean I was wearing a different hat yesterday', I remonstrated, and got away with it.

The judge then asked a court official how many more witnesses were still to be called, and refused to allow so many. So a solicitor went in to address the bench on our behalf, asking if those who had been subpoenaed as witnesses and had been attending the court for days without being called should still be allowed their expenses. The judge ruled that they should, whereupon we all put in claims for rather extravagant expenses, and merrily queued up for the cash reimbursement – which in some cases, I heard, actually meant unusual solvency for its recipients.

Terry Chandler's next Old Bailey date followed his arrest with other former C100 activists for his participation in an anti-military demonstration at the Greek embassy on 28 April 1967. He was charged with affray and assaulting a policeman. But the supposed evidence for it was so flimsy that the charge was eventually dropped. Meanwhile, Terry was on bail, awaiting a judge-and-jury trial at the Old Bailey. Again he insisted on conducting his own defence and again introduced an unheard-of ploy. Somehow he got hold of the complete list of names and addresses of forthcoming jurors for that session, and, since prisoners had the statutory right to challenge any juror they suspected of prejudice, he decided to have an opinion-survey carried out on all of them, using the Eysenck personality test.

I was one of Terry's supporters who were given a jury list to follow up, and, posing as a social assessment surveyor with a named list for statistical balance, I called on the listed citizens and interviewed them. Some of their attitudes really shocked me. For instance, a family man with a kindly manner actually held that homosexuals should be sentenced to flogging. Ideas like that. Often asked whether I agreed, I found it difficult to keep up the pretence of being impartial. In the end there were hardly any respondents whom I felt I could recommend to Terry for the jury.

On the first day of the trial, Terry took a card-index into the dock with him, and rapidly consulted it as each potential juror was called. The reports of all his other surveyors having apparently been similar to mine, Terry challenged each prospective juror, one after the other, until there were hardly any left spare in the building. This unprecedented situation was suddenly the leading item of news on radio and television, and eventually resulted in the judicial court procedure being limited to seven challenges against the jurors picked by chance.

There was, admittedly, an element of creative gamesmanship in our public-spirited civil disobedience.

MAIDEN PARLIAMENTARY SPEECH

It must have been about 1965 when I addressed the House of Commons (illicitly, of course) from the public gallery. Several members of the former C100 had contacted one another, including me, with a conspiracy to go to the House one particular evening and make speeches at 10-minute intervals, opposing Harold Wilson's support for L B Johnson's reactionary policy against North Vietnam.

Realistically, this meant just the opening words of such speeches, since there were always stewards – that is, official chuckers-out – on duty in the public gallery, waiting to pounce on anyone daring to utter. (What red-letter days in their humdrum working lives must such rare occasions have been!)

Although the chamber, spread out below us, was three-quarters empty, and I was inured by this time to attracting public notoriety and arrest, I found this assignment the most daunting I had ever embarked on. The first of the unofficial speakers from the gallery was a courageous middle-aged immigrant from eastern Europe, and as he was being dragged out by the stewards I looked at my watch and decided I would be next, exactly ten minutes later, if no-one else pre-empted me – as I rather hoped would happen.

My instinct was to stand up to make my speech, but, in order to maximise the time before the stewards reached me, I had already positioned myself in the very centre of one of the long pews and reckoned that it would save a few more seconds if I were to remain seated as inconspicuously as possible, while speaking in the loudest voice I could manage without standing.

Drafting my opening sentence in my head, I took a deep breath and suddenly heard myself project my voice with my statement. The sprinkling of MPs below all looked up to the gallery, for the second time that evening. Also for the second time, the stewards sprang into action. It took them two or three seconds to locate my voice and push into the pew to reach me. My gender probably saved me from being too roughly handled, and I was trundled, rather than dragged, down the steps, out of hearing of the susceptible ears of our elected legislators.

Taken to a comfortable sitting-room, which I later discovered was the waiting-room generally used by MPs' chauffeurs, I was gradually joined by former C100 colleagues – but only the women. The men were taken to a less comfortable room, and were not treated as well as we were. For instance, on asking to go to the lavatory, we were taken to one that was used by women MPs, whereas the men were simply told to hold it!

I was captive from about 7:15 pm to midnight, and it was like a gradually burgeoning party, filled with chatter and laughter. A highlight of it came at 9 pm when one of the prisoners who had had the forethought to secrete a transistor radio into her handbag switched it on so that we could hear the Radio 4 news. Sure enough, we featured in it, but were described inaccurately as 'a group of young people'. In fact we were of varying ages – the two oldest participants being in their sixties. At the time, however, the word 'young' was used as a synonym for irresponsible. (The next day I complained to the BBC about this misreporting, but received no response.)

We were released, without charge, after the House rose at midnight. The authorities obviously wished to avoid giving us the publicity of appearing in court, but it was a minor punishment to keep us prisoner until the last trains and buses had left central London. Somehow I did manage to get home – there may already have been a few night buses to the suburbs by that time – but even had I been stranded till morning, the thrilling experience and lifelong memory of my curtailed maiden speech would have made the lack of a bed well worth it.

Seated a few places away from me in the public gallery there had been a woman Labour supporter I recognised from the Shaw Society. The next time I met her I rather expected her to congratulate me on my parliamentary speech, but on the contrary, she told me she was disgusted by my disrespect for Parliament. She never spoke to me again.

Our secret non-gunpowder plot may have been provoked by a widely reported gobbet from L B Johnson: when asked to explain Wilson's submissive reaction to America's bombing the hell out of North Vietnam, the President's memorable reply (supposedly off the record) was said to be 'I've got his pecker in my pocket'. At the dawn of the present century, G W Bush, planning his invasion of Iraq, could have said the same about Tony Blair.

For access to the House of Commons, those of us interested unofficially in attending any of its proceedings were expected to waste time queueing outside with the tourists, but I found a way of jumping the queue. I used to address an envelope to a particular MP, seal it, and take it to wave at the policeman in front of the queue. He immediately let me in to take the supposed letter to the mail-room, then I simply turned from there into the lobby.

MEASURE FOR MEASURE

Planning a modest London sit-down in 1961, a group of us decided it would be an additional embarrassment to the Metropolitan Police if, with no magistrates' courts on duty, those arrested were to refuse bail, thus putting overnight pressure on police-station cells. In the event, however, only a dozen of the men did refuse bail, and, since most women felt the need to prioritise their domestic roles, I was the only woman left in custody.

Sex segregation of prisoners was strictly adhered to, and it was apparently *de rigeur* that they must have a guard of the same sex. The woman on duty in the police-station that I was taken to was called a 'matron', but this was an insult to hospital matrons, however severe. She had more in common with a Nazi concentration-camp commander – but with only one prisoner on her hands. In her eyes I was no doubt far more deserving of retribution than the usual drunk, and having me under her thumb must have made it a red-letter night for her. Not only did she relieve me of all my possessions apart from clothing, she offered me no food or drink, and she put me in a cold cell with just one thin blanket that stank strongly of vomit. At about 2 am she came to the end of her spell of duty, not to be replaced, so I was woken and transported to another police-station with a female officer, where again I was alone of my sex. The date of my incarceration was 6th September 1961. I know, because I have unearthed a souvenir I kept of the occasion – the dated luggage-label that identified my confiscated possessions, with a full list of them written on the reverse. Next morning, reunited at the magistrates' court with my fellow male transgressors, I was envious to learn that they had enjoyed a cooked breakfast.

A year later, Leslie likewise experienced imprisonment (aged 68), spending a week in H. M. Prison, Maidstone, because he had refused to pay a civil-disobedience fine. He said the other prisoners (who called him 'Pop') were all amazed that he declined freedom at the cost of a small fine. But the only hardship to him, he told me, was the lack of brown bread! Certainly, the experience would be nothing to him at all compared to life in the trenches, all those years before.

One Saturday afternoon in 1968, I was arrested at a sit-down outside the American Embassy in Grosvenor Square protesting against their military action in Vietnam, when the authorities forestalled the bail problem by setting up a magistrate's *ad hoc* court for the summary processing of offenders. Having found me guilty, the *ad hoc* magistrate read out a list of my previous convictions, complete with locations and dates, and asked me whether it was correct. I had no idea, so could only reply 'Well, if you have the details in front of you, I suppose it must be.' I was in fact astounded that the archival personal information had been accessed so quickly, for it was my first intimation of the portentous electronic revolution.

The C100 comprised, as it were, a great university education, and though it existed formally for no more than three or four years, its spirit lived on, through individual enterprises and various small groups.

A provincial location for nuclear rockets provoked a group of local residents to bring, in protest, a replica of a rocket from there to the seat of government, staging a public march to carry it to London. The intended target was either Westminster or an appropriate ministry in Whitehall, but since access to either area would obviously have been prevented, I was asked about an alternative destination. I suggested the Imperial War Museum, to indicate that the weapon was obsolete, and the dummy was accordingly deposited at the main entrance of the museum.

STATE SURVEILLANCE

We were always aware, of course, that our telephone lines were tapped by the authorities, so we were careful to avoid saying anything on the phone that we did not want them to know.

Once, when about twenty local youngsters had to get to a police court in Norfolk one morning, because they had taken part in an illegal demonstration at the Marham RAF base (of which we conducted a spoof auction!), I ascertained which of them had motoring parents willing to take them to the court and asked whether they had spare car-seats, which I then allocated to those without transport. I telephoned everybody, giving them a location – the junction of two minor roads, where the cars and passengers were to meet at 8 am. There was no need, of course, for me to say what it was about, and the authorities must have imagined I was organising an illicit demonstration, for I was amazed and amused to find our meeting corner packed with police, awaiting us. We simply waved them goodbye.

Telephone tapping was one thing, but the 'bugging' of

one's home quite another, and it did not occur to me that MI5 would take me seriously enough to bug my flat. But apparently they did. A shortage of telephone lines at that time meant that neighbours had to share lines, and immediately after being put on a shared line I had been told I was to be given a solo line again! Then one day a man came and said he had come to repair a fault in my telephone receiver, of which I had been unaware. He did something to the instrument, said I should have no more trouble with it, then left. Though it seemed unusual for a telephone mechanic to have a public-school accent, I thought no more of it.

Some time later, when my telephone receiver genuinely sprang a fault, an ordinary telephone mechanic came to repair it, and asked me what the small electronic device was that was stuck underneath the receiver, as he had never seen one like it before. And what should he do with it? Still not putting two and two together, I replied 'I suppose you'd better just replace it'.

After the housing department of the Greater London Council had made an offer to Mrs Birch for the purchase of her house (as related in chapter 5), and I moved to Stanstead Grove, I received several phone calls purporting to come from British Telecom, saying they needed to get the telephone receiver back from Dalmain Road. As the instrument was only an obsolete model that people were throwing away, I had simply left it behind, but the callers persisted they must get access so as to recover the phone. The house now being 'tinned up', I finally told them to contact the GLC.

It still did not enter my head that my flat had been

bugged by MI5 – in fact I would not have thought I was worth their assembling a dossier on me – but a few years later I was reliably informed by a young man in Integroup (a local club for integrating gay and straight people, to which we both belonged) that indeed they had done so.

He was gay, and though he was rather right-wing we gradually became friends. At first, he told me, he had been horrified by my political opinions and lack of respect for the law – and as a civil servant seconded to a job that allowed him access to MI5 files, he had, out of sheer curiosity, speculatively requisitioned 'the pink dossier on Barbara Smoker'. (Pink, he said, signified Highly Subversive.) Questioned by MI5 staff as to why he required the dossier, he replied that he had some additional material for it, whereupon he was told he would have to give explicit details 'as this dossier is now dormant'. So although he never saw it, he had proved it existed. Now, he said, he had come to realise who I was: obviously Graham Greene's 'Aunt'! Having enjoyed Greene's racy eponymous *Travels*, I could not altogether resent the unlikely hedonist persona.

Since I would never go in for any violent or vandalising activity, this over-reaction on the part of British security, presumably widespread during the Cold War, must have wasted a vast amount of time and public money.

PORTON DOWN

The notorious governmental research establishment at Porton Down, near Salisbury, was set up as long ago as 1915, in response to Germany's production of mustard-gas for use against the British, and has remained operative ever since for the experimental production of poison-gas, which, originally chemical, later became also biological. It has been described as 'the UK's most secret military research base' – but state secrets are not water-tight for ever. This one was leaked fifty years ago, and we learnt that its obscene products were being tested on animals. Two of my pet hates thus came together: war-mongery and vivisection. (The addition of religion would make it an alternative malevolent trinity.) I therefore decided to join some young successors of the former C100 who planned to visit the base in protest.

It was a huge site, containing isolated white huts in a sea of grass, and was surrounded by a high wire fence with yellow Ministry of Defence warnings of 'DANGER!'. My young companions managed to climb or penetrate the fence, but as climbing it would not be possible for me and cutting it was against my principles, I simply stood defiantly beside the wire while they were inside. After some minutes, a sort of tank on the horizon began to slowly move in my direction, rather like a robot. No human driver being visible, it felt rather spooky as the tank came right up to me. A small aperture opened in its side and a sort of nozzle poked through.

Due to my past experience on demonstrations, I imagined it held a lens to take a photograph of my face, and my instinct was to turn away. But that seemed a cowardly, guilty reaction, so I looked straight at the aperture. Only later did I realise that, since photography would obviously not require all that artifice, the nozzle must have been a conduit for the ejaculation of poison-gas, containers of which would be stored in the tank. The purpose of the whole charade was presumably to scare me.

A television documentary about Porton Down was shown on BBC4 last year (on 7 December 2017), with cruel shots of conscious sheep (suffering from induced anthrax) and rabbits (infected with some other induced disease). Since Britain has never yet used poison-gas in warfare, the government is able to pretend that this research is merely in readiness for defence, but that would not require ejaculating tanks. Besides, the TV programme made it clear that the whole enterprise is on an industrial scale – which, alongside the physical cost to the sheep and rabbits, must impose a colossal monetary cost on the British taxpayer.

CHAPTER SEVEN
MULTITASKING

IF VARIETY is the spice of life, my life has had its full share of spice. The closest I have ever been to a steadfast career was my 25-year presidency of the National Secular Society, which, together with the funerals and other commitments that stemmed from it, deserves a chapter in itself. That will be chapter 8 – just as sedition monopolised chapter 6. Other activities are lumped together here.

One of my selected part-time jobs was with the Institute for the Study and Treatment of Delinquency, to which a friend in the Shaw Society introduced me. For eight years I did some sporadic office work for them, but was mainly working on *The British Journal of Criminology*.

Later, through the National Secular Society, I met Cecil Turner, who, together with his Swedish wife, owned a small book-publishing firm, Bachmann & Turner, and he tried to persuade me to work for them. Refusing, of course, to succumb to regular employment, I accepted his proposal on a part-time basis, ghost-writing and copy-editing for some of his authors and writing blurbs for their book covers. Reciprocally, Cecil published my illustrated book of irreligious verse, *Good God!*.

PHONETIC ALPHABETS

In the Shaw Society in the early 1950s I met the octogenarian Russell Scott (nephew of C P Scott, the renowned editor of the *Manchester Guardian*), who was a great enthusiast for phonetic alphabets, with particular interest in the German *Sprechspur* (Speech-tracing), which, he had discovered, was taught in schools in Westphalia. Seeing the need for something similar for the English language, he had corresponded with Shaw on the subject. He would talk about it incessantly, rather like the Ancient Mariner, and I was one of the few people who listened to him with real interest and caught his enthusiasm. Eventually I took over from him the secretaryship of his diminutive Phonetic Alphabet Association, and increased the membership a little. I used to write frequent newsletters for its members, mainly about the competition that was set up by the Public Trustee in 1959 in furtherance of Shaw's alphabet bequest, and I published details of it in the *New Statesman* and the *Competitors' Journal*.

For a couple of years I spent many hours each week in the British Museum reading-room (which later moved to the new British Library), researching phonetic alphabets designed for English from the 16th century onwards, and intended to write a book on the subject. In fact, I built up a sizable card-index for it, but never got around to writing the book – only writing articles and giving talks on it. However, my research meant that I knew enough about it to understand what Shaw wanted – and why – so that I was able to brief Mr Milner-Holland, QC, on behalf of the Attorney General, who stood *ex-officio* for Shaw's testamentary wishes, which were challenged in the Chancery Division in February 1957 by his ultimate residuary legatees as invalid. But we lost the case, apart from a derisory out-of-court settlement – which paid for a bi-alphabetic edition of Shaw's play *Androcles and the Lion*, as he had stipulated.

GROUPS

In the later 1950s, as regional humanist groups began to sprout up around the country, I joined together with a few like-minded people to set up one in my home locality, the borough of Lewisham. Inaugurating it in 1960, we named it the South-East London Humanist Group and organised monthly discussion meetings and other activities. After some years I found myself in the combined roles of its secretary, chairman and general factotum. A number of deaths among the members then caused a further decline in attendance at meetings, whereupon, having more prominent activities on my hands, I announced dissolution of the group unless any existing member was willing to take it on. There was one: a new member named Bronwen Cobell. With assistance from her husband Denis, she brought the group to life again. Then, for many years, Denis himself served as its diligent secretary. The group is still active – but now, after 58 years, I am the only surviving founder member.

In 1969 I co-founded a group to promote a more radical penology campaign than the existing campaign for prison reform. I chaired its inaugural meeting, and (as mentioned in chapter 1) we christened it Radical Alternatives to Prison. Why, we asked, did there have to be such a large prison population in this country? Eventually, our most successful plea was for the alternative of community service orders, but their implementation still lags behind that of most European countries.

The smallest committee I ever served on (if we discount the innumerable committees of one!) comprised just three BHA members: David Pollock, Anthony Chapman and myself. Its aim was to work out a fairer and simpler basis for the financial benefits of charity status than the existing charitable categories established in law as long ago as 1603 – when the most important aspiration was deemed, of course, to be religion. Having met several times, the three of us finally decided that the one practical way to avoid any subjective value judgments would be to grant automatic tax-exemption to every non-profit-making organisation. But this spot-on solution cut no ice with our legislators, who still accept the unbalanced four-centuries-old criteria for charity status.

MID-LIFE MULTITASKS

Activities kick-started in the early 1970s (my middle years from birth to the present day) were to prove the most intensive and long-lasting of my life.

It was in 1972 that I was first elected President of the National Secular Society, having been its Acting President for some months in the previous year, and it led to my officiating at non-religious funerals (see chapter 8).

Later that year I was commissioned by the educational publishers Ward Lock Educational Ltd to write the booklet *Humanism* in their 'Living Religions' series for secondary schools, putting the positive alternative to all religions. Though I had no experience of writing for teenagers and was not looking for a job alongside my secularist lectures, press-releases, journalism, funerals, and so on, it was always against my nature to turn down any new opportunity, so I accepted the Ward Lock invitation. Whether I succeeded in adapting my writing style to the target readership is questionable, but anyway I think it is better to write slightly above the heads of young people than to underestimate them. My main difficulty was finding appropriate illustrations, especially one for the front cover. The authors of other titles in the series were able to use for their front covers spectacular colour photographs of temples, mosques and cathedrals – and Conway Hall hardly seemed to compete. But when I was almost ready to take my typescript to the publishers a Sunday newspaper colour-supplement provided me with a good cover illustration. It was a photograph of the Earth, taken from one of the satellites then orbiting the planet, and I captioned it 'the focus of humanism'.

On delivering my corrected proof to Ward Lock's editorial department, I was dismayed to be told that its fifty-six pages exceeded the maximum length by four pages. I protested that it was exactly the same length as the booklet on Hinduism, which was already in print. The reply, however, was that the Indian author had obdurately refused to allow a word of his masterpiece to be cut, and, while it was impossible to omit Hinduism from a series on world religions, the omission of Humanism would be quite acceptable.

Already on my deadline, there was no time for proper pruning, so I simply chopped four pages out of the section on morals! Forty-six years (and six editions) later, that amputation has been more than replaced – by an extra 24 pages. As for the rest of the book's long publishing history, that can be held over till chapter 10.

The word 'humanism' having been appropriated meanwhile by some progressive religious sects, it has rather lost its edge. I am often advised therefore to rename my book 'Secular Humanism', or even 'Atheism'. But it would be confusing to do so, since its essence is basically unchanged, so I have merely added a sub-title: 'for inquiring minds'.

In the early 1970s, a few of us from the NSS formed an official deputation to the BBC, opposing the discriminatory editorial policy that excluded any non-religious contributor from the weekday Radio 4 item *Thought for the Day*. (I was to return to this issue thirty years later, and will deal with that venture in chapter 9.)

My long-term support for homosexual equality led to an invitation from the erstwhile Gay and Lesbian Association to join its panel of vice-presidents, alongside my presidency of the NSS, and over the years I also became a vice-president of various other organisations. Two of them which still accord me this honour are the Shaw Society and the New Zealand Association of Rationalists and Humanists.

Towards the end of 1971 – in retrospect, a most productive year – I brought out a humanist diary for 1972 and the following year, and sold it alongside a Yuletide card which was one that I had designed and published for the Shaw Society a few years earlier. It portrayed a grumpy-looking GBS dressed as Father Christmas, and was captioned with wording that Shaw himself had used on a card sent to his friends one year: 'Courage, friend! We all loathe Christmas; but it comes only once a year and is soon over.' It also served as one of the illustrations required for the Ward Lock booklet.

During each November for several years I used to advertise that card in the *New Statesman* as an 'anti-Christmas-card', and later I began building up a whole series of cards with mocking Christmas cartoons, marketed as 'Heretic Cards'. Each year I added one or two new designs, totalling more than forty, and I still receive a few orders for them as well as running a seasonal Heretic Cards stall at Conway Hall. For several years I was inundated in November and early December with orders by post for the cards, and had to get friends to help me pack them. In more recent years, however, I have sold them mainly at meetings.

One of the earliest designs remains the most popular of all: it depicts the traditional crib scene with Joseph announcing 'It's a girl!' – trumped by one of my nephews with his alternative wording, 'It's twins!'.

When the National Council for Civil Liberties (now Liberty) advertised for volunteers to monitor the fates of protestors in local magistrates' courts, I volunteered. At one such appearance in the Greenwich court, a group of young people was remanded on bail – but one member of the group was not to be granted bail because no friend or relative had come forward to stand surety for him. Impulsively, I stood up and told the magistrate that I owned a freehold house in Catford and was willing to offer it as warranty for the defendant's next court appearance. This was accepted. The young man looked surprised, and I spoke to him outside the court, saying I trusted he would not let me down. He was very grateful and kept to the bail terms.

FUNERALS

In the second half of the 19th century, Annie Besant had been by far the most popular celebrant for secular funerals, and when I followed her as a secularist funeral officiant a century later, someone kindly gave me copies of three of her texts as a guide. But they were far too florid to be of any use to me. Instead, I relied for my template on Harold Blackham, and even his wording needed some modernisation.

When I began officiating, I also took over the fee of five guineas that Harold used to charge, reduced to £5 on the currency decimalisation. Today the fees are invariably in three figures, the past four decades or so having seen non-religious funerals gradually become big business – not only for members of the secular humanist movement but for members of the general public. When I began tutoring BHA volunteers in 1972 on how to conduct funerals, I managed to give my pioneers the necessary confidence in a few hours, but now celebrants are professionally trained and monitored over an extensive course. Basically, a good funeral officiant is born, not made. The most important attributes are: first, being a good listener and secondly, having a gift for words as well as the thespian ability (in the absence of a mike) to project one's voice.

In the forty years from 1970 to 2010, I must have conducted more than a thousand funerals, in addition to which I was conducting non-religious wedding ceremonies, gay commitments (before the era of civil partnerships or the later same-sex marriage) and baby-namings. Some of my ceremonies were shown in television programmes, including a multiple commitment event for eleven gay couples, a wedding ceremony in Chessington Zoo, and a funeral filmed for BBC2 in 1996.

For most funerals I relied on interviewing those close to the person who had died, but occasionally the interviews were with those who were terminally ill themselves. I also had to oversee the order of ceremony and whatever music was required, contact the people wanting to give eulogies, and write it all up, making photocopies for the mourners. There were periods when it became virtually a full-time job.

During the 1980s and early '90s, before the pharmaceutical and medical professions discovered how to combat AIDS, a disproportionate number of funerals I carried out were for young gay men. One that I remember in particular was for an AIDS victim who, having come from a fundamentalist Christian background, had renounced religion to become an atheist. He was then rejected by his parents, but when he died they sought a court injunction against his having the non-religious funeral he had requested. For six months his body was kept in a morgue, but eventually we were given the legal go-ahead for the funeral I conducted. (Though I invited the young man's parents to attend it, they declined.) He had bequeathed his money to the NSS, but a five-figure bite from it was swallowed by the lawyers.

I conducted about twenty times as many cremations as burials. Partly because the mounting pressure on land in the southern counties for the living, let alone the dead, made burial expensive, cremation had been gaining ground (sorry about the pun) since the nineteenth century, especially among the non-religious. In the Catholic Church, however, cremation was prohibited until 1963, and is still traduced, while practising Muslims renounce it absolutely.

CHRISTIAN TAKEOVER

Though most crematoria were municipally owned, being built and maintained by the local authority, they were largely taken over by Christians – not by purchase, but by the simple expedient of getting a bishop to come and bless them – and religious icons prevailed in the crematoria chapels.

In one owned by my own local authority, Lewisham Borough Council, there was at that time a huge brass cross on the wall behind the catafalque, and I was told it could not be removed for non-religious funerals. Even my suggested compromise of covering the cross with a cloth was refused, as that was the prerogative of high-church ritual during Lent.

Then the non-religious mother of an infant candidate for cremation said she really hated having that instrument of torture hanging over her baby's coffin, and she offered to pay for its removal. She was levied a three-figure surcharge for this, as I was told it needed five men to lift the cross down and replace it (yes, even including its replacement for the next Christian funeral) – and the men would have to be paid danger money.

I kept up a protracted correspondence with the appropriate council committee about this religious discrimination, and the press took it up, whereupon the local Unitarian minister joined forces with me, but to no avail for several years. Eventually, the Council changed its corporate mind and decided to substitute permanently for the existing monstrosity a small, easily dismountable cross – though this decision was made less for the sake of the many non-believers than for the politically correct sake of possible Hindu and Sikh immigrants. An even more persuasive argument was probably the fact that the infamous brass totem could be sold at a lucrative estimation.

The then secretary of the S E London Humanist Group, Denis Cobell, who still officiates at that crematorium, tells me that the chapel attendant there always removes the dismountable cross for him automatically – hanging it up in the vestry, where it serves as a convenient coat-hanger!

GLC CANDIDATE

I decided to stand in Lewisham East as an 'Abolish the GLC' candidate in the Greater London Council election of

May 1977, and managed to obtain the requisite number of citizens' signatures. My motive was primarily anarchistic, on the grounds that there were too many levels of government; secondarily, I still felt a personal grudge against the GLC for its attempt to get me evicted from my rented home in Dalmain Road some twelve years earlier.

Denis Cobell, who shared my anarchistic viewpoint, offered to be my agent. It was really a bit of missionary impertinence, as there was no possibility of the ballot tellers being overworked on my account, so I would not have bothered about leaflets had not the local press wanted to take photographs of me canvassing. That meant I had to hurriedly produce a few leaflets, whereupon Denis got his eight-year-old daughter Sally to push some of them through letter-boxes in their locality. Then, at the post-election count in the town hall, he claimed every possible spoilt ballot paper as a vote for me.

Following the declaration, each candidate was allowed to deliver a speech, in the order of votes obtained. There were six candidates, of whom I came sixth, with 127 votes. I was therefore scheduled as the sixth speaker – but the communist, who came fifth, was gentlemanly enough to let me speak ahead of him. (This would now be denounced as sexist.) The burden of my speech was that though I had obtained the fewest votes, I was the moral winner, since the low turn-out of the electorate could only mean apathy, which I interpreted as a vote for abolition: I had thus won hands down.

Nine years later, Margaret Thatcher succeeded where I had failed, and in April 1986 the traditional County Hall building lost its incumbents. Another twelve years on, however, Labour virtually overturned the abolition of the GLC by inaugurating the Greater London Authority (GLA). This comprised London's first directly elected Mayor together with the separately elected London Assembly – supported by more than 600 permanent staff!

On 15th July 2002 they moved to a dumpy (though presumably functional) new building, City Hall, adjacent to Tower Bridge on the south bank of the Thames – directly opposite the former speakers' site at All-Hallows, where I used to mount the atheist platform every Thursday. When I attended a function at City Hall as a guest years later, I was pleased to note that at least its huge windows sported solar panels.

JURY SERVICE

I was never summoned for jury service until October 1977, at the age of 54, and then it was for the Old Bailey. I hated the idea of having to determine people's guilt or innocence, like Jehovah separating sheep from goats (Matt. 25,32), especially as the purpose of it is to facilitate punishment decided by a professional judge. As for imprisonment, I thought it justifiable only for criminals such as homicidal maniacs who are too dangerous to be left at large. Even then it should be made as pleasant as possible to compensate for their loss of liberty. The belief that punishment somehow wipes out guilt, or repays society, is not rational: it is superstition.

I spent two weeks in the jurors' canteen, drinking endless

cups of coffee, between visits to one court after another for inclusion in the formation of jury panels. Each time, I was rejected by the defending counsel in one of the seven objections permitted before each juror is sworn in. The barristers have nothing but one's appearance to go by, but it seemed to me that they accepted all young people and most men, while tending to challenge middle-aged white women unless dressed unconventionally. I therefore deliberately wore my most conformist clothes each day and put on a severe facial expression whenever called for a case. And it worked. I was immediately challenged by the defence every time except twice – and even in those two cases was belatedly challenged.

In one of them it happened as soon as I said I wished to affirm instead of taking the religious oath – though I would have thought that that indicated a beneficially independent mind. On the other occasion I got even further before being challenged and had given up all hope of a reprieve, having seen judges disallow belated challenges.

This judge, however, had the effrontery to ask me, while the affirmation wording was being located, whether secular affirmation would be binding upon my conscience. He presumably thought that though no-one would dare break a Bible oath, secular affirmation might be a trick to escape divine wrath. Not only was he exposing the medieval straws in his wig, he was in clear contravention of the Administration of Justice Act by failing to put affirmation on the same footing as the oath. I had already begun reading out the words of the affirmation by the time the defendant's objection was made, but the judge illicitly allowed it, much to my relief.

I wrote up the whole experience for the *Freethinker* (December 1977), and was upbraided by a lawyer in its February issue for my abdication of social responsibility, since 'someone has to decide on the guilt or innocence of persons accused'.

Though jurors were admonished not to talk about their cases outside of their jury-room, the chatter in the jurors' canteen was about little else, and during my fortnight I heard a lot about the current cases. One of them was an indictment of attempted murder, the accused having clearly tried to kill his wife. His trial came to an end during my second week, and seeing one of its jurors in the canteen I went up to her and asked 'I suppose you found him guilty?' 'Oh no,' she replied; 'he was so nice, and she was a real bitch.' So much for the mandate of juridical evidence.

If charged with a serious crime of which I was actually guilty, I would opt for trial by jury – but not if I was innocent of it.

EUTHANASIA

In the late 1970s, the Voluntary Euthanasia Society, founded in 1935, changed its name dramatically to Exit and commissioned *The Guide to Self-Deliverance* for publication. Written by a libertarian doctor, it detailed a method of painless suicide involving drugs and a plastic bag, and the Exit secretary, Nicholas Reid, handed the typescript over to me for editing.

It was an illicit publication, as the statute that had decriminalised suicide in 1967 introduced the crime of assisting a suicide, which incurred a prison sentence of up to 14 years. However, since this English statute did not cover Scotland, the pamphlet was openly sold there but only furtively in England.

Serving on the Exit committee from 1980, I was elected its chairman the following year, and succeeded in reversing the name change to the original VES. We committee members were all separately interrogated by the police about the *Guide*, but followed the advice of our solicitor to refuse to answer any question, however innocuous.

In September 1984 I attended the international euthanasia conference in Nice, organised by the World Federation of Right-to-Die Societies. There were more than 700 participants from nineteen countries, and I was among the listed speakers in two of the three main sessions: the legal and the ethical. Coining the phrase 'the Art of Dying', I was quoted as saying that the rational choice of one's own time, place and manner of death, so as to round off life's unique pattern with dignity – neither prematurely not belatedly – can be seen as an art form.

Though the VES constitution limited the chairmanship to four years, this restriction was waived in my favour so as to cover 1985, the year of the Society's golden jubilee. As well as giving talks and writing articles on voluntary euthanasia, I organised the special VES anniversary meeting and compiled a symposium on the subject for publication (as noted in chapter 10).

I remember several of the 1980s euthanasia case-histories,

one of which was a singular case that hardly merits the prefix 'eu'. It concerned a young man with a death wish. Like all other VES members, he aspired to dying at the time of his own choosing, but unlike them he did not want to postpone it until incurable disease or disability made life intolerable. Though healthy and intelligent with a comfortable life-style and excellent prospects, he believed that all human life was a curse, so decided to pre-empt his future by committing suicide flamboyantly.

He asked his mother which was the best hotel in London, and, not realising his intention, she told him she thought it was Claridge's. He then booked in there for a couple of nights. Ordering a sumptuous dinner-party (the last supper?), to which he invited a few friends, he paid the bill for it by cheque on his inadequate bank account, knowing that he would be dead by the time it bounced. After his guests had left the hotel, he killed himself painlessly – successfully using the *Guide to Self-Deliverance* method.

He left a handwritten letter addressed to the manager of Claridge's – not apologising for the trespass, but thanking him for the superlative terminal care he had received! I felt sorry for the hotel staff and still more for his mother – punished for inflicting life upon him.

Meanwhile, Nicholas Reid, manning our office, kept receiving telephone calls from true euthanasia candidates, often screaming down the phone. Many of them were physically unable to procure their own death, and of course the law prevented anyone from helping them do so. Then an eccentric man named Lyon, elderly and blind, offered to step in and assist the suicides by monitoring the drug-and-bag method, and Nicholas was relieved to pass the harrowing cases on to him. While the air-tight plastic-bags were completing the job, Lyon would take a rest outside, usually to eat a banana – which was his main diet.

Somebody must have informed the police, and Lyon and Reid were both arrested and charged with criminally assisting suicides, the former being remanded in custody, the latter on bail. It was a full year before their trial, during which I visited the old scallywag in Brixton prison (taking in some bananas) as often as I was granted a visiting order – and I realised how badly the incarceration was affecting him. Meanwhile, the name Lyon inspired some punning public protests by young supporters against his being 'caged'.

The trial judge decided at the outset that as Lyon had already spent a year in prison, he might be freed immediately on bail if there was someone available to take responsibility for him, and at the end of the first day's hearing called on me, asking if I was willing to do so. Though I did not relish the job, I felt I could not delay poor Lyon's release by refusing to take it on, so I collected him at the end of the day, and he wept with relief. All I had to do was feed him and see him safely to his lodging for the night, as he would be collected from there the next morning by the lawyers. But he was even more of a handful than I had expected. For instance, his method of crossing a busy road was simply to step out into the traffic waving his white stick aloft. I managed to set up a rota of three of our supporters to act as his guardians for the rest of that week, but none of them was willing to repeat the experience the following week.

Nicholas obviously did not expect a custodial sentence, as he travelled to the court by motor-cycle on the last day of the trial, but he was jailed for a year. His accomplice, given the same sentence, was immediately released, having already served the time on remand.

OVERSEAS TOURS

In 1983 I attended an international atheist convention in Helsinki, and there met Madalyn Murray O'Hair from Austin, Texas. She founded American Atheists Inc. and was known as 'the most hated woman in America', because of her abrasiveness as well as her atheism – which almost everyone in the USA took to be synonymous with communism. She told me that when one of her members died having bequeathed his unique library of rare antiquarian books to her organisation, his pious widow fulfilled the literal terms of his will by burning the lot and mailing the ashes to the Atheist Center. Every Easter Madalyn held a large atheist conference at various American locations, where she made a lot of money, and she invited me to the next one as a speaker, with all expenses paid plus the gift of a month's Greyhound bus-pass at the end of it, supporters' homes all over the country where I would be welcome to stay, and arrangements for appearances on radio and television. Needless to say, I accepted the invitation, and my account of the tour can be found in the *Ethical Record* under the title 'A Primitive Country'.

Twenty-one years later, Madalyn, her second son Jon and

her granddaughter Robin were kidnapped, for their money, and finally murdered. A Texan senator declared it would be a waste of resources for the FBI to investigate the fate of an atheist family, and the authorities dragged their feet over it for five years, allowing the clues to evaporate. That senator's name was George W Bush.

Eventually, however, the three bodies were located, exhumed and identified. The story filled several pages of the *San Antonio Express*, and a friend of mine living there, knowing of my past association with Madalyn, collected the cuttings for me. I wrote it all up for the *Ethical Record*, where it appears in two instalments (March and April 2007) under the title 'The Most Hated Woman in America'.

Another extensive speaking tour was to India (from the end of 1989), organised by an Indian member of the NSS council of management. It included a month's railway pass and the membership of two international atheist conferences. As with the tour of America, I also stayed in some supporters' homes.

A second, much shorter, visit to India took place in 1998. Apparently my 25-year presidency of the NSS as successor to Charles Bradlaugh had made my name famous among atheists in India, where Bradlaugh is still revered. So the mass atheist organisation Dravidar Khazhagam invited me by telephone to inaugurate a forthcoming atheist event in Tamil-Nadu. At first I declined, but on the third importunate phone-call I said 'All right – but only for the weekend'! The idea of undertaking so long a journey for so short a visit rather tickled me.

My humanist colleague Malcolm Rees, who had lent me his spare room after my house-fire (see chapter 9), offered to go with me, and he was a great help in carrying things, as well as socially. We flew to Chennai (formerly Madras) on Thursday 29th January, and returned to London on the Monday. However, the organisers did not allow for the short time available by reducing the number of jobs lined up for me. I rarely got to bed before the early hours, and it was still dark when I was woken in the morning. It was the most exhausting few days of my life.

Friday night we spent on an all-night train to Thanjavur, where the whole town centre was decorated with bunting printed with the black-and-red Dravidar Khazhagam logo, and the next day we visited a most impressive educational complex for 5,000 girl students from four-year-olds to post-graduate level, and I was roped-in to present prizes.

Sunday was the day of the convention, preceded by an exhilarating parade with acrobatics and tricks with fire, at-tracting a crowd of more than half-a-million. It took two hours to pass the high dais on which I stood, during which a caparisoned elephant trunked a garland round my neck. (I still have it on my sitting-room wall.)

The convention itself took place in a huge auditorium with an assembly of 12,000, and went on until 1am. In my speech as the main speaker I compared and contrasted our two cultures, especially with regard to religion, and com-plimented the host organisation on its impressive social projects. I then launched their newly published compila-tion in English entitled *Why I Do Not Believe in God*, and also officiated at a quadruple secular wedding, in which each of the four ex-Hindu couples comprised one low-caste and one high-caste partner.

Atheist rally in Tamil-Nadu, south India

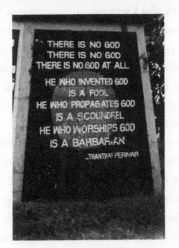

Prayer by an Indian atheist

CHAPTER EIGHT
NATIONAL SECULAR SOCIETY

OF ALL the organisations for causes that I joined in the 1950s and '60s, the one that was to prove really life-changing for me was the National Secular Society – especially through working with its Secretary, Bill McIlroy.

Bill was a refugee from the fundamentalist Orange culture of Northern Ireland. He once told me that in his youth he had even thought of converting to Catholicism to escape from it, but realised in time that he could be an atheist instead. Since that resulted in social intimidation, he migrated to England, and his detestation of religion led him to the NSS, where his zeal appealed to the old guard, who handed him the reigns.

Although he and I were very different in temperament, he saw that our shared militant opposition to despotic religion made me a useful ally. So when, in 1971, the hands-on NSS President, David Tribe, stood down to return to his native Australia, and a few weeks later the elderly woman who succeeded him resigned over a dispute, Bill asked me if I would like to take over the job. He said it would open a lot of doors to me – and so it did. The one condition he stipulated was that I should be willing to conduct members' funerals, and I was happy to take that on – as Acting President until elected at the 1972 AGM.

My presidential NSS predecessors included the trenchant polemical writer Chapman Cohen, whose term of office spanned 34 years, from 1915 to 1949. Mine was to fall short of that by just nine years.

Meanwhile, my humanist mentor H J Blackham, on reaching retirement age, had left the London area for the Welsh Marches. (He told me that it was in order to escape from seventeen committees!) Until then he had been the main funeral officiant for members of the Ethical Union – which he had renamed the British Humanist Association. (Now, 55 years later, it has again been renamed, as 'Humanists UK'.) Though HJB still came back to London for the more important BHA funerals, most requests for them were now handed over to the National Secular Society, since the new BHA secretary, Kenneth Furness, refused (much to Bill McIlroy's scorn!) to do them.

Discovering that I was now officiating at funerals, Kenneth asked me if I would take over the training of a few hand-picked BHA members, and in 1972 I did so, as the first BHA funerals tutor.

GENESIS OF *HUMANISM*

Besides funerals, there was another venture for which I remain indebted to Kenneth Furness, and it has proved to be one of the most important achievements in my life. It was the genesis in 1972 of my booklet *Humanism*, as a school textbook for teenagers.

This resulted from the post-war resolve of educationalists to substitute more universal Religious Education for the prevailing Religious Instruction in local-authority schools. In response, the educational publishers Ward Lock Educational decided to launch a ground-breaking project for secondary schools: their 'Living Religions' series of illustrated paperbacks, comprising one booklet for each major world religion, to be written by a believer in that religion.

When some of the first booklets in the series were already in production, someone must have pointed out to Ward Lock that humanism, which had become increasingly popular in universities and widely recognised as the one positive moral alternative to all religions, was conspicuous in its absence from the projected 'Living Religions' series. The British Humanist Association therefore received a request from the publishers to recommend an author for a booklet on humanism, targeted at teenagers.

I happened to meet Kenneth Furness on an outing, and maybe he recalled that it was I who had written the BHA recruiting leaflet headed 'What is this Humanism?' – already then in use for some fifteen years. Anyway, he asked me there and then if I would be interested in taking on the Ward Lock project. I can only guess that none of the prominent members of the BHA at that time had volunteered to write it – a guess based on my experience of other elected committees before and since (for example, that of the Voluntary Euthanasia Society twelve years later, when a projected book of theirs likewise fell into my lap).

At my ninetieth birthday party in Conway Hall, Andrew

Copson, CEO of the BHA and leading spokesperson on secular humanism, said that he had first come across the word (in our sense) from my book at his secondary school, where the Ward Lock 'Living Religions' series was in use. I heard recently that copies of the original edition are selling for considerably more than the price of the latest superior version! (To my mind that is ridiculous).

Another publishing venture of mine was humanist diaries for 1972 and 1973, containing sixteen pages of secular humanist interest, which I brought out and marketed together with my earliest Xmas cartoon greetings cards, which I called Heretic Cards.

LONGFORD

Lord Longford, who had set up a private committee on pornography in the mid-1960s, published its reactionary conclusions under the title *Pornography: The Longford Report*. Not only did it take a stand against popular moves to liberalise the censorship regarding so-called 'obscenity'; it additionally proposed abolishing the legal defence of anything being 'in the public good'. Though the Longford Report was trounced by book reviewers, the only public protest meeting against it was called by the NSS – filling Conway Hall on 3 October 1972.

I remember gathering a batch of ivy-leaves to represent the biblical fig-leaves, which I took along to the meeting for members of the audience to wear, and I chaired the meeting. Our main speaker was the writer Brigid Brophy. She handed her text over to us and we published it as a pamphlet (priced at 10p), for which I wrote the Foreword.

I had initially met Longford years before, when he was still Lord Pakenham. At that time I had a part-time job with the Institute for the Study and Treatment of Delinquency, which invited him to give a lecture on imprisonment. Listening to the noble lord's address, I came to realise, with some dismay – since by then I had firmly renounced the Christian idea of 'justice' for 'sin' – that he actually believed in punishment for its own sake, not just for deterrence and rehabilitation.

Years later, I saw Longford one evening on the Charing Cross concourse, presumably waiting for his homebound train. Though I would never deliberately cut an acquaintance, I decided not to approach him as he had the reputation of never recognising anybody, even members of his own family. But he did recognise me, and came up to me with the greeting 'Still bashing God?'

He then said something really funny: 'I suppose you despise me because you were a cradle Catholic and I am only a convert.' If I did in fact despise him, it would certainly not be for that reason. However, his thinking so was probably due to his belonging to the aristocratic social circle in which Catholic families were, apart from any intrusive Irish blood, generally recusant – that is, those, such as the Duke of Norfolk, who had remained faithful to the Church throughout penal times. In my memory, people who were (or pretended to be) from a recusant family used to pronounce 'Holy Mass' to rhyme with 'arse' instead of 'ass'.

In fact, my own family's religion went back no further than Grandma Smoker, who, after Catholic Emancipation, was a young convert of Cardinal Manning.

PARLIAMENTARY INQUISITION

By 1980 a parliamentary select committee (the Education, Science and Arts Committee), was set up to look into
the curricula in secondary schools, and although the terms
of its reference did not mention religious education, the opportunity to deal with it was immediately recognised. Two
of the nine MPs who volunteered to sit on it were therefore
religious extremists, but the humanist Chris Price, MP, was
elected to the chair. He decided that the committee could
not probe religious education unless the witnesses appointed
from several mainstream Christian sects were balanced by
nominees from the BHA and NSS; the BHA nominating Dr
Harry Stopes-Roe and the NSS me. Every witness had to
provide a written memorandum, published in a supplement
to *Hansard*, before appearing in person to be questioned
orally; but whereas the Christians were all accorded individual visiting slots, the two non-believers had to appear
together, though questioned separately.

Our memoranda were very different in style and empha-
sis – Harry's being academic with abstract concepts, calling
for a widening of RE to include various 'life-stances', whereas
mine was down-to-earth and simply demanded the removal
of the present religious bias with its statutory compulsion
and subsidy. So as to avoid any possibility of being at log-
gerheads in person before the committee, we negotiated to
narrow the gap between us on the BHA's proposed life-stance
education, which I was willing to accept as long as it was not
left in the hands of the existing RE teachers, often trained in
teacher-training departments rooted in Christian theology.

The time allotted to our joint oral evidence was from 5 to 6pm on 22 June 1981, the previous hour being reserved for the Catholic Church – in the person of Cardinal Basil Hume.

Arriving purposely an hour early so as to hear the cardinal's evidence, I was directed to the largest of the committee rooms, where the scene mirrored the one shown in a large 19th-century painting that hung on the carved panelling. Members of the committee took their places on high-backed gold-crested green leather chairs around three sides of the large table, the fourth side being earmarked for the witnesses. An outer ring of similar chairs was taken up by two-dozen journalists and BBC personnel with their recording apparatus.

Cardinal Hume took his place at the table, flanked by two aides – one a bishop, the other a lay expert in religious education – and the committee members took turns to question him, very gently. I was not surprised that Patrick Cormack was sycophantic, but was surprised when Stan Thorne, who had previously been a member of the BHA, began 'Like the chairman, I would like to thank you for answering questions this afternoon, particularly as my wife thinks that we should be answering your questions!' But this excessive politeness was reassuring to Harry and me, awaiting our turn.

The cardinal vindicated the need for religious education and church schools by citing the malaise of the consumer society, race relations and disparity of wealth – but was not asked why he trusted religion to mitigate these problems when it had done nothing but exacerbate them throughout history.

As the hands of the clock neared 5 pm, the chairman brought the session to a courteous close, and invited Harry and me to take our places at the table. Some members of the press left at that point, but some stayed, and the BBC carried on their recording – a part of my evidence being broadcast on Radio 4 the following Sunday.

We were questioned cannily on the membership figures of our respective organisations, suggesting that they hardly justified our presence there. We contended that it was the proportion of the general public holding opinions similar to ours that was more relevant, but this only elicited a demand for statistical details that we did not have at our finger-tips – though the cardinal had cited vague statistics without details being demanded. When Harry answered one question in the form of another question, he was told simply that he was there to answer questions, not to ask them – though when the cardinal had similarly put one of his replies in the form of a question, he had been given a courteous answer. And the following day Archbishop Runcie was likewise soft-soaped.

Harry and I were each questioned on points in our printed memoranda, and at the end we were told we would be expected to send in supplementary memoranda with detailed supporting references that we did not have to hand in the committee room – but this was actually to our disseminating advantage.

Regarding the size of our public support, I was able, in my supplementary memorandum, to quote the statistics of religious affiliation in England and Wales from the Gallop Poll of May 1980, giving 13% RC and 12% atheist or agnostic

– a gap of only 1%, though the cardinal had not been asked to justify his presence. As for his reliance on moral issues to establish a need for religions in schools, I was able to cite official statistics showing that in penal institutions the proportion of RCs exceeded twice the representation in the population at large, while unbelievers were under-represented.

GREENHAM COMMON

As partial compensation for my permanent exclusion from the BBC's daily radio comment slot *Thought for the Day*, I was invited in 1981 to present a personal comment on BBC1 television, on any subject of my own choosing. This was no doubt expected to be atheism or secularism, as I was known primarily at that time as President of the NSS. But in the event a more pressing concern of mine was the forthcoming deployment on British soil of American cruise missiles with nuclear war-heads. Though their expected date of arrival was a state secret, it was leaked by a source which had previously proved reliable, and by chance it happened to be the very date arranged for my free-speech comment on television.

Therefore, with the help of a knowledgeable local friend, Sid Goldstein, I prepared a hard-hitting speech on that subject. Only a few minutes before my arrival at the Television Centre the news broke of the almost simultaneous arrival of cruise missiles at an American air-base in Berkshire, and I got the producer of my spot to show me the wording of the news item that made my proposed speech newsworthy. I was able to hand over my typewritten speech for an autocue to be prepared for the recording, and my spectacled eyesight was good enough to read it without difficulty at a fair distance, thus minimising discernible movement of the eyes. And it went well.

However, this nuclear occupation of Britain by the United States remained *in situ*, with the connivance of Parliament, for the next nine years – until the end of the Cold War in 1990.

All that time, it was opposed by the counter-occupation of a bivouac of young women protestors on nearby Greenham Common, on behalf of their (mainly unborn) children. It is one of the great historical stories of democratic protest. Although I was never one of the Greenham Common campers – after all, being in my late fifties onwards, I was well past the age for it – I did visit the site on odd days in support of them.

Middle-aged maverick

EGGS ARE NOT PEOPLE

Clinical treatment of human infertility through IVF became widely available in this country in the early 1980s, and the Warnock Committee proposed a government-sponsored bill to legitimise embryo diagnosis and selection for the avoidance of congenital defects and also for medical research on the spare zygotes.

Although, as an ultra-cautious sop to the religious lobby, the Warnock Report proposed a statutory limit of a meagre fourteen days from fertilisation, it provoked a fanatical outcry from many church leaders, parliamentarians and other public figures, in defence of 'little human beings' – which in fact at that stage are nothing but an undifferentiated cluster of cells (about the size of this full-stop).

Enoch Powell being induced to sponsor the absurdly titled Unborn Children (Protection) Bill, this, put to a free vote at its first reading on 15 February 1985 in the House of Commons, actually prevailed by a massive 238 to 66 votes – indicating either incredible biological ignorance in our legislative body or its craven reaction to the religionists.

Before the Bill's second reading, I therefore wrote a factual article for the *Freethinker* on the subject, entitled 'Eggs are not People'. This was then reprinted as an illustrated pamphlet, which the NSS distributed individually to every MP – after which the Powell Bill was unexpectedly defeated.

ISLAM RAMPANT

In May 1986, an article of mine opposing state-funded Muslim schools was published in the *Freethinker*, and the

same issue carried an article entitled 'Islamic Terrorism' –
more than twelve years before the twin towers terrorist atroc-
ity in New York.

Muslims were apparently told that their greatest enemy
was secularism, so, taking me to be its representative and
therefore the chief opponent of Islam, Muslim students in
various polytechnics used to request open debates between
me and an imam with the gift of the gab. (The polytechnics
were later renamed universities, as though on a par with Oxford or Cambridge.)

During my 25 years' presidency, I therefore addressed
innumerable sessions of under-graduates on secularism, and
the meetings were officially sanctioned by the faculty. But
they attracted only Muslims. These included a minority of
Muslim women students, who sat on one side of the aisle
while all the men scrabbled for seats on the opposite side.
This prompted me to write beforehand to each college faculty
– none of whom ever showed up at debates – asking them to
support my opposition to segregated seating; but their reply
was always that I should put it to the vote at the start of the
meeting. When I tried this, the whole audience voted for gender segregation – even the women. (One of them explained
to me later that they would otherwise have been groped!)

I was invariably treated with ultra-politeness, and was occasionally asked whether I objected to a video being made of
the proceedings. I made no objection to this, but noticed that
the students sometimes saved money by switching the apparatus off when the eloquent imam finished his speech and I
began mine. Realising that I was enabling extremist imams

to provide videoed sermons for future use, I wondered if I should refuse these invitations, but thought it would be interpreted as pusillanimity.

The meeting was generally told by the imam that democracy was wrong, since it was the will of Allah that mattered, not that of human beings. And the meeting's highpoint was often the declaration that Britain was likely to become the first Western caliphate. On one occasion a single English non-Muslim student attended the meeting; he came up to me afterwards and said 'I didn't realise it was as bad as this'. And in subsequent years it often transpired that British-born Muslim terrorists had actually been 'radicalised' in a British university, not just a mosque or madrasa.

Needless to say, whenever a vote was taken at the end of any of my Muslim college debates, the result was a foregone conclusion.

I frequently warned politicians (mainly Labour) of the danger of their expedient appeasement policy towards Islamic fundamentalists, and I campaigned against the unchecked Muslim oppression of their own girls and women. After carrying out an investigation into the misogynous Muslim community in Hackney and the parallel Hassidic community in Stamford Hill, I reported in print on the way that both communities denied their girls any secular scientific education and integration with their English neighbours. I was denounced, to my surprise, as racist and anti-Semitic, by Ken Livingstone (then leader of the Greater London Council), in his weekly column in the *Evening News*. I wrote to the paper in my own defence, saying that I took

issue with religion, not race – but they could not find any
space for my letter.

A similar public denunciation was later made, likewise
unjustifiably, against Livingstone himself, and I wrote to him
saying that, while the accusation against him was obviously
absurd, I could not help a feeling of *Schadenfreude*.

A number of liberal Jewish people in the Stamford Hill
area told me that their Hassidic neighbours not only refused
to speak to them or allow their children to do so, but actually
referred to them as 'goyim', 'English' and even 'anti-Semitic'.
Hassidic girls are brought up with the idea that they must
always be submissive to men and that their role in life is to
fulfil the biblical injunction to 'increase and multiply'. Because of the Rabbinical ban on family planning, the average
number of children in Hassidic families is seven; but when
I described this policy as socially irresponsible, I was told
there was no such problem: everyone in the world could fit
on the Isle-of-Wight!

MUSLIM EXTREMISM

When Muslim zealots held a big march in London on
27 May 1989, demanding not only extension to Islam of the
prevailing British common-law crime of blasphemy but the
immediate execution of Salman Rushdie for that alleged offence in his panoramic novel *The Satanic Verses,* I stood alongside the route holding a home-made banner that read, simply,
'Free Speech'. A few yards away I saw Nicholas Walter and
his wife Christine, holding a larger home-made banner with
the same two-word slogan. (Free minds think alike!)

Physically threatened by a surge of marchers yelling 'Kill, kill, kill!', I was saved from serious injury by, I think, a plain-clothes policeman, and was then quizzed by a newspaper reporter and quoted next day on the front page of a tabloid paper. Nicholas and Christine were pushed over and slightly injured.

On that occasion, 123 of the Islamic demonstrators were arrested for injuring policemen – generally regarded as a custodial offence – but all were released the following morning without charge, obviously in accordance with a misguided Home Office directive.

FREE SPEECH

Muslim politicos apparently learnt from us the wording 'Free Speech' for use as a slogan – but it was a case of a little learning being a dangerous thing, for the new Islamic slogan that soon began to appear on demonstrations read 'Free Speech for Muslims'. I laughed aloud when I first saw it, but it is no laughing matter that the aspiration of free speech could be so misunderstood as to restrict it to those of like mind. In fact, it can only be meaningful in the application to both sides of a contentious issue. As Orwell wrote in *Animal Farm*, 'If liberty means anything at all it means the right to tell people what they do not want to hear.'

In September 2005, six quite mild cartoons of Mohammed (though one of them did depict him with a bomb tucked into his turban) appeared in a Danish journal. Though there was no adverse reaction to them for about four months, Islamic extremists then began publishing exaggerated versions of them in various Muslim countries, provoking widespread outrage and many murders.

Consequently, the motion chosen for the Oxford University Union Debate of 25 May 2006 was 'Free Speech should be moderated by respect for Religion'. Although I was no longer an elected representative of secularism, someone must have remembered me, as I was asked to be the secondary opposition speaker – supporting Fleming Rose, the Danish editor who had published the original Mohammed cartoons. Since there was a seven-figure bounty on his head, security arrangements for the debate were heavy, everyone being searched on the way in – but it was a full house.

For the first time, I found myself on the winning side! We won by 129 votes to 59. Had the word 'Religion' in the motion been replaced by any other abstract noun, we would

Speaking at the Oxford Union debate, 2006

have won by 188 to nil. Suppose the word had been 'Science', the motion would read 'Free Speech should be moderated by respect for Science'. No-one would have voted for that – least of all a genuine scientist.

GUESTS-OF-HONOUR

During my long NSS presidency I met many important people on the secularist wave-length, especially guests-of-honour at our annual dinner, when I was privileged to spend the evening with them. Several then remained friends. They included (in chronological order): Dora Gaitskell, Helen Brook (of the Brook advisory centres), Phyllis Graham ('the nun who lived again'), Dora Russell, Lord Houghton, Maureen Duffy, Denis Lemon (victim of the blasphemy law), Edward Blishen, Renée Short, Michael Foot, David Yallop,

With Dr Jonathan Miller

Peter Atkins, Benny Green, Jonathan Miller, George Melly, Larry Adler and Polly Toynbee.

In 1986 a decision was made to use the names of our most eminent members and supporters as signatories to a letter intended for publication in the broadsheet papers. It was taken from an article I had written in opposition to the segregation and indoctrination of children in denominational schools – later cannily christened 'faith' schools – with public subsidies grossly multiplied by successive governments, creating educational ghettoes for many immigrant children.

The letter was circulated to the intended signatories for approval, then recirculated with amendments. But a printers' dispute at the *Times* led two or three of our politically-minded signatories to threaten removal of their names if the letter were to be published in that paper. Though I was pleased to see it with the 23 celebrity sponsors' names in the *Guardian* of 9 July 1986, publication in the *Times* would have made more impact for this momentous cause – and I still cannot forgive those who precluded it on behalf of a temporary trade grievance. Today, the government still sanctions a rapid extension of religious schools throughout the country.

Part of the letter read as follows.

Sir, – We are very concerned about a dangerously divisive factor in our educational system: the large number of voluntary-aided denominational schools that segregate children according to their religious background... This may seem, superficially, a progressive step, in line with current trends towards multi-racial education and bilingualism; but in fact it would mean for many children – especially girls – of immigrant families almost total isolation from the host community and from ideas at variance with those of the home background. This would not only be a disaster for these youngsters personally, it would also inevitably build up for future generations a greater degree of animosity and violence than we have seen even in Northern Ireland. There, children are segregated on grounds of religious background only; in this case there would be the additional divisive factors of race, skin colour and sex...

In the name of equity, however, it is manifestly impossible for the state to refuse Muslims and Sikhs the same right as Christians and Jews to state-subsidised schools of their own. How, then, can this looming social tragedy be averted without blatant discrimination? Only by Parliament legislating without delay to gradually phase out subsidies to denominational schools of every kind. Besides encouraging integrated schooling, this would make good economic sense: at least 85 percent of the capital cost and 100 percent of the running costs of voluntary-aided denominational schools are financed from the public purse, and this dual system of education is notoriously wasteful...

We cannot deny that a parliamentary decision to phase out subsidies to denominational schools needs considerable political courage... and demands an all-party determination to grasp the nettle.

Yours faithfully,

(Prof Sir) Alfred Ayer; (Dr) Cyril Bibby; H J Blackham; Edward Blishen; Christine Bondi; (Sir) Hermann Bondi; Brigid Brophy; (Prof) Bernard Crick; Govind N Deodhekar; Michael Duane; (Prof) Lionel Elvin; (Sir) Raymond Firth; (Lord) Houghton of Sowerby; Madan Nohan Kalia; Ludovic Kennedy; (Prof) Karl Lofmark; George Melly; Naomi Mitchison; (Dr) Joseph Needham; Christopher Price; (Lord) Raglan; Barbara Smoker; (Lord) Ted Willis. (c/o The National Secular Society).

BRADLAUGH HOUSE

Conway Hall having been subtitled 'Humanist Centre', in the closing years of my NSS presidency I aimed to complete that concept in practice by bringing together all the main humanist organisations under the one roof. A perfect opportunity for this came about when the adjacent building at the north-east corner of Conway Hall came on the market, and I succeeded in persuading the NSS committee to buy it.

Harold Blackham and Nicolas Walter were both in favour and a doorway was cut into the party wall. The British Humanist Association, the International Humanist and Ethical Union, and the Rationalist Press Association all became tenants of the NSS there in 1994, and Michael Foot came to perform the opening ceremony, naming the building Bradlaugh House, in honour of Charles Bradlaugh.

Sadly, however, just nine years later the BHA decided to move away, losing the NSS a large part of its income. The NSS therefore decided to move into Conway Hall

Still causing trouble

proper and sell its own adjoining premises. My ecumenical dream thus came to an end.

NSS SECRETARYSHIP

Following Bill McIlroy's resignation in 1977 as the NSS General Secretary, Jim Herrick filled the post for the next two years, and when he resigned, due to pressure of work, I approached Terry Mullins as a likely successor.

I had at first met Terry when trustees of the British Humanist Association, of whom I was one at the time, were going on tours of university humanist groups, and at Stirling we were each assigned a student guide. My guide was Terry, a mature student, whose Irish-cockney humour – including 'gallows humour' – kept me laughing the whole time. He was quite open about his gayness, and joked about it. And he was an uncompromising atheist. So when the NSS secretaryship fell vacant, I thought of Terry – his wit as well as his commitment – and wrote asking him if he would like to step into the job. He accepted with alacrity, and I persuaded the NSS committee to appoint him.

Terry held the job of NSS General Secretary for sixteen years, and on the strength of it bought a large house at a bargain price from a fellow humanist, who made it a condition of sale that Terry should run it as a humanist community house. This he did: mainly, but not exclusively, with gay humanists as tenants.

He was quite obsessive about avoiding waste – for instance, always switching off unwanted lights – and if any piece of equipment broke down he would usually devise a Heath Robinson sort of way to continue using it rather than buy a new one. In addition to his house, however, he enjoyed one other item of expensive but important ownership: his old banger. And it was part of his generosity to me personally that he would often drive me in it on long journeys – including a visit to a convent near Liverpool when my sister Paula was terminally ill there.

He was an active joiner of societies and groups committed

to his various interests and causes, of which the Ethical Society at Conway Hall was probably the most important – especially its Sunday evening chamber-music concerts, which he loved – and he continued to attend the lectures and concerts there regularly, even after succumbing in the last few years of his life to severe mobility problems caused by a rare neurological disease similar to Parkinson's. Other organisations in which he was active included musical fellowships, the Shaw Society, the atheist campaigning London Secular Group, the Campaign for Homosexual Equality, and his local Residents Association. Aside from his astute input for practical decisions, his humour and clever witticisms caused a lot of laughter at meetings and also contributed to his many friendships, comprising an amazingly varied circle.

When Salman Rushdie became the victim of an Islamic death threat, Terry placed a copy of *The Satanic Verses* in the window of the NSS shop in Holloway Road. I pointed out that it could result in the window being broken, to which Terry responded 'Well, we're insured'.

I relied very much on his practical cooperation in my NSS presidential role, but he was no more suited to the emerging computer age than I was, so it was clear as he approached the age of 65 in 1996 that he would have to retire and be succeeded by someone younger with digital acumen and skill. However, as the NSS always paid him a low wage, Terry had not, despite his frugal lifestyle, finished paying off the mortgage on his house, so he asked to stay on for another couple of years. But he received no support for this. I felt myself that it was indeed time for him to go, but suggested that the NSS could resolve the situation by paying him on retirement a thousand pounds for each year he had been employed as its hard-working secretary. While this was no more than he deserved, since we had always underpaid him, the rest of the council of management decided to drastically reduce such a 'golden handshake', and, though he managed financially, he never really forgave them.

He was succeeded by Keith Porteus Wood, who provided the NSS with its first website and, making it clear that he did not intend to be a mere support to the President (as Terry Mullins had been), upgraded the title General Secretary to Executive Director.

Meanwhile, at the next NSS AGM, my re-election as President was contested by a former vicar, Dan O'Hara. And he was well supported – mainly by ardent socialists, some of whom had already opposed my political liberalism, although, like the NSS founder, Charles Bradlaugh, I was a *radical* liberal. And they had already set up a Socialist Secular Society.

Dan won the 1996 presidential election. I did not really mind, however, feeling that my innings of 25 good years at the helm was long enough. But Dan had assumed that, like me with Terry Mullins, he would be running the show, and he was not satisfied with playing second fiddle to Keith. So he soon resigned.

The following year I was urged to stand again for the presidential election, but I declined. After all, I was now well past the biblical final retirement age of three-score years and ten. My old friend Denis Cobell then succeeded O'Hara as president, being willing to fill the role of Keith's supporter.

He did so competently for ten years, until stepping aside in 2006 in favour of vice-president Terry Sanderson.

By this time Keith's percipient use of the internet had expanded the Society's sphere of influence, engendering expansion of the presidential role, and Keith and Terry S. reigned jointly for the next eleven years – dynamically.

They introduced significant changes to the character of the Society, which thenceforth dropped its opposition to religious creeds, regarding them as merely personal, so as to concentrate on opposition to public religious privilege. To inaugurate this retrenchment, they drew up a 'Secular Charter' – and I have to admit, howbeit reluctantly, that this more focused approach has pragmatic advantages. Furthermore, through exploitation of the rapid electronic revolution, they expanded the orbit of the Society internationally (in spite of its name), often in cooperation with the International Humanist and Ethical Union, and with considerable success.

Terry Sanderson's retirement in 2017, and Keith's choosing to move over to the presidential chair, then opened the way for Stephen Evans to be appointed the next Executive Director – his manifest communicating ability as the prevailing NSS campaigns director having decisively proved his fitness for the top job.

My house in Stanstead Grove, Catford

CHAPTER NINE
PETERING OUT

I LIVED in my lovely house in Stanstead Grove, Catford, for thirty years, and let out rooms rather than waste time and energy on uncongenial work. Instead, I continued reading, lecturing, writing, broadcasting and generally throwing my weight about.

Until, that is, one December afternoon in 1995, when I stupidly set fire to the house – a few weeks after letting the insurance lapse.

HOUSE FIRE

Having no central heating, I had always kept a paraffin heater in the hallway, mainly to avoid frozen pipes. That day, in semi-darkness because the ceiling light-bulb had given up the ghost, I re-filled the paraffin tank – forgetting that it was already almost full.

Of course I knew it was proscriptive to fill the heater while it was alight, but I had been getting away with this misconduct for three decades. Not on this occasion, however. The oil overflowed and flared up. I ran upstairs for a prophylactic fire-blanket I kept there, and threw it down over the heater – only to see the blanket itself catch fire.

Should I run to fetch buckets of water, or should I phone for the fire brigade? Realising that either strategy could well trap me in the burning house, I ran out and shouted to my neighbours to phone the fire-station for me.

One of them did so, then joined me at the front gate, waiting with me for the fire appliance to arrive. Woefully I watched flames and smoke rising to the roof of my house. However, it was the jeopardy of the adjoining houses on both sides – especially the one where there was a bedridden woman – that worried me most of all.

It was a great relief when I heard the fire appliance approaching – but (horror!) it failed to stop. It was on its way to another fire.

It was only another two or three minutes, however, before the one allocated to me arrived, and the firemen soon managed to get the conflagration under control. One of them sat me in their vehicle and, noticing I had slightly burned my right hand, bandaged it, gave me a bottle of sterile water to pour over it, and asked me for phone numbers of local friends or relatives. Getting no answer from my sister Celia's number, he left a message on her answering service. I was able to tell him that my friend Malcolm Rees would be working in the Lewisham public library, so he phoned a message to him there.

When the firemen were satisfied that the fire was completely extinguished, they insisted on taking me to Lewisham Hospital, where, just as I was being discharged from A & E, my sister and her husband turned up in their car. My brother-in-law asked me where I would like to be taken, and my reply,

'To the library', must have sounded funny. But it was a good decision, for Malcolm not only took me home to his flat, he gave me the use of his spare room and telephone for the next three months, at the end of which Lewisham Borough Council assigned me the tenancy of my present flat – the only one, I was told, that I would be offered. I then sold my partly gutted house, as it stood, for refurbishment.

I am so lucky that the council flat I was allocated was not one of the 1960s campus high-rise flats, but happened to be one of four in a two-storey pre-war block on an ordinary quiet road. A few years later the Council, faced with austerity, sold a widespread area of its council estates to a new housing association, Phoenix – of which I am now therefore a tenant.

THOUGHT FOR THE DAY

In the early years of my NSS presidency, I had led, to no avail, a deputation to the highly respected national public communications service, the British Broadcasting Corporation, in protest against the exclusion of non-believers from the daily Radio 4 item *Thought for the Day*. Under that title, each morning from Monday to Saturday, in the middle of the peak-audience *Today* programme, some social issue is dealt with by a believer (in any religion), but never by an atheist, agnostic, or secular humanist – as though a legitimate opinion on social issues has to entail religious belief. It is therefore presented as a religious programme. And where else does the BBC allow unquestioned personal comment? As for the word 'Thought' in the title, I would contend that it would be more, not less, appropriate in the absence of religious creeds. But the programme's discriminatory editorial policy remains a thorn in our side, almost half-a-century later.

In 2002 – that is, some thirty years after the failed NSS deputation to the BBC – it was decided that the time had come to sue the corporation under the Human Rights Act 1998 for the blatant injustice of *Thought for the Day*. In order to initiate such a law-case, the NSS needed an up-front plaintiff who could claim to be personally affected by the unethical exclusion, and I was asked to fill this role. Ironically, I was interviewed about it on the *Today* programme.

A comment in a red-top paper was that the secularist demand for access to *Thought for the Day* was like cooks presuming to take over a gardening programme. This was applauded as a witty analogy – but it was obviously a false one. A far more pertinent analogy would be the permanent exclusion of vegetarians from a cookery series. If the name were *Prayer for the Day*, we would not want to take part in it, but it is gross impertinence to deny us Thought.

Introducing me in their initial legal complaint to the BBC, the instructed solicitors for the NSS wrote: 'As the author of books on humanism and freethought and a contributor to television and radio, she would be, but for this editorial decision, a likely prospective contributor to *Thought for the Day*.' I had to write a supposed specimen contribution to the programme, and also attend several consultative meetings in our barrister's chambers while the preliminaries went ahead for a judicial hearing. Before this reached court, however, the Legal Service Commission cancelled our public-funding certificate. This meant we had no alternative but to withdraw the case, since the BBC had limitless funds for it from the statutory TV licences, whereas, had we lost and heavy costs been awarded against us, the NSS could well have been left penniless. Justice has always depended on Mammon.

However, the NSS gained some good publicity, including almost a full page of comment in the *Sunday Times*, and the campaign was supported by many important people, including Michael Foot, Harold Pinter, and Richard Dawkins. In the end, there was also the 'own goal' of Mr Alan Bookbinder (then head of BBC Religion and Ethics) who boasted, in a published statement, that the BBC had succeeded in 'fighting off the atheist lobby' – as though it was the BBC's mission to uphold the bias of religious creeds rather than reflect society as a whole.

Seven years on again, the BBC apparently launched an internal inquiry into *Thought for the Day*, for I have come across a cutting about it that I kept from *The Sunday Times* dated 19 July 2009. It is a personal comment by the journalist Rod Liddle, and reads as follows: 'The BBC Trust is now to consider the matter, which is good news for Barbara Smoker, the former president of the National Secular Society, who has been banging on about this for years and used to write me scary letters when I worked for the BBC.' The BBC, however, apparently contrived, yet again, to justify (at least to their own satisfaction) this continued corporate discrimination.

Since May 2018 a monthly protest rally organised by the South East London Humanist Group has confronted BBC personnel, presenting them with more 'scary letters'.

Handing in another 'scary' letter at Broadcasting House

MEDIA

My presidency of the NSS gave me plenty of opportunities for coverage on radio and television. One of my more important radio breaks was a talk, 'Why I am an Atheist', recorded in 1985 by the BBC World Service, and twenty years later, on 19th September 2005, I was one of three apostates interviewed in a Radio 4 programme 'Losing my Religion'—not my choice of title. A part of my contribution was pleasingly then selected for *Pick of the Week*. But television had largely overtaken radio for public recognition in Britain.

A mere sound-bite of mine on television really caught on. When Mother Teresa was hailed by Malcolm Muggeridge as a living saint, I referred to her on the BBC TV programme

Question Time as 'a sacred cow'. Years later, a radio producer invited me by phone to represent the atheistic viewpoint on a forthcoming discussion programme, but as it was not a slot that grabbed me, and in any case I was no longer the official representative of the NSS, I replied that there were younger people who could now speak for atheism and secularism. 'Yes', was his response, 'but you are the one who called Mother Teresa "a sacred cow"!'

Whether likewise for the memory of that sound-bite or something else, I was chosen in my dotage to take part in two really notable TV series, for both of which I was favourably reviewed. One was the London Weekend Television programme *After Dark*, featuring seven disputants who were locked in a real-time debate from Saturday midnight until about 3 am on the Sunday. My programme being at an Easter weekend, the opening theme for discussion was the Christian doctrine of Jesus' bodily resurrection, this then broadening to miracles in general. Towards the end of the broadcast, the presenter said to me: 'Perhaps you will eventually revert to the religion of your formative years.' 'That, of course, is quite possible', I replied; 'it's what is called "senility".'

The other TV engagement I was pleased to accept was a programme in the second BBC2 series *Living with the Enemy*. Its fly-on-the-wall format required me to spend a week in 1999 under the roof of 'the Pioneer Team'. This was a coterie of evangelical Christian proselytisers who had federated about a hundred happy-clappy churches and several social projects in the 'New Church' movement.

Filming took place all day, every day, in various religious

situations, and as much as sixty times the film footage was shot as was going to be broadcast. Though some good solid argument was available, the editing policy preferred personal confrontation to anything that smacked of intellectual debate. It also featured, as a 'running gag', an absurd charade that happened at the time to be a national news item. A young woman had claimed hysterically that her amalgam tooth-fillings had miraculously transmuted into gold during a 'Toronto blessing' conducted by the leader of the Pioneer Team – which affected to support her delusion. Camera shots inside her mouth took up an inordinate part of the film, but I was glad that at least the perfidious editing did not delete my reaction to the story. I asked why, even if she was confident about the transmutation, she ascribed it to God, rather than to the more appropriate Tooth Fairy!

I felt quite sorry for the woman who had made such a fool of herself, but when I later scrolled the BBC's Online Forum about the programme (comprising 214 messages), I found to my horror that a number of the contributors – all presumably educated and computer-literate – actually seemed to believe in alchemy.

It was gratifying that new media opportunities still came my way in spite of retirement from almost all my offices. There were also the unexpected TV repeats when, switching on my TV set, I occasionally had the shock of seeing myself; but I was really amazed when a friend in Holland rang me one day to say she had just seen me in *Living with the Enemy*, with the addition of Dutch sub-titles! I wrote to the BBC claiming Dutch royalties, but to no avail.

BBC THEOLOGY

On Holy (Easter) Saturday, 2008, the BBC featured on its television channel BBC2 a spectacular hour-long peak-time 'documentary' film on the Turin Shroud (the supposed burial sheet of Jesus Christ). It mainly comprised special pleading to explain away the 1988 carbon-14 dating of the cloth that had established it as a medieval forgery. The rust-coloured splashes (previously identified as paint) were now not only described unequivocally as blood, but the actual blood group was specified! Needless to say, it had to be the most rare of the human blood groups, which happens to be AB – and I wondered how many viewers recalled that, for the same reason, the AB group was likewise accorded to Tony Hancock in the radio and TV classic comedy *The Blood Donor*.

The next day I wrote to the producer, politely asking which laboratory had tested the blood, so that I could follow it up and find out perhaps whether the DNA was analysed at the same time. If so, I wondered if it cast some light on the presence of a Y chromosome. This would be necessary, of course, for Jesus to be born male, though a parthenogenic pregnancy, in the alleged absence of a human father, would normally have to result in a clone of the mother (such as Dolly the sheep).

Although I enclosed a stamped addressed envelope with my letter and sent a copy to the head of religious broadcasting at the BBC, I never received a reply. Nor was there any public acknowledgement of their having received any such requests or complaints.

Before leaving the subject of Easter, I cannot resist

quoting a wonderful letter that was published 55 years ago in the *Middlesex County Times*. 'Easter, with us once again, should bring sobering thoughts to those fanatics who, in opposition to God's Divine law, advocate and campaign for the abolition of capital punishment. Many Christians must often, like myself, contemplate the terrible consequences to mankind if capital punishment had been abolished some 2,000 years ago and Our Lord had been unable to sacrifice his only begotten son on the Cross to save us all.'

DE-BAPTISM

On the very first page of this memoir, I denounced the abusive practice of infant baptism, and in my dotage I decided to hold a 'de-baptism' ceremony for myself at a party for atheists, and to publicise it. Obviously, it could only be a tongue-in-cheek gesture, but it would make a valid point.

In preparation for the ceremony, I composed suitable wording for my inscribed de-baptism certificate. At the party I signed it and had it witnessed – then made photocopies of the certificate.

I was interviewed on the BBC Radio 4 programme *Woman's Hour* about my de-baptism (I think the word was my coinage), and this broadcast resulted in my receiving letters from ex-Christian listeners who wished to arrange a similar ceremony for themselves. They included victims of Protestant infant baptism, while my original certificate contained the injunction 'I wish to be excluded from future Roman Catholic statistical claims, except for the statistics of apostasy'. I therefore produced a more ecumenical de-baptism wording, which the National Secular Society used on a batch of printed pro-forma certificates for sale. Here it is:

DECLARATION OF DE-BAPTISM

After due deliberation, I ....
having been subjected to the rite of Christian baptism in infancy (before reaching the age of consent), hereby publicly revoke all implications of that rite and any pledges made on my behalf. I renounce the Church that carried it out, and, in the name of human reason, reject its creeds and all similar superstition – in particular, belief that a baby needs to be cleansed by baptism from alleged original sin and the evil powers of supposed demons. I therefore wish to be excluded henceforth from enhanced claims of church membership.

Signed: .... Date: ....

Witnessed by: ....

EULOGIES

Over the years I have been the subject of some very kind, not to say flattering, articles. One of them, published in *The Guardian* on 28 July 1983, was a full-page head-swelling profile by Polly Toynbee. Another appeared in the Spring 1992 journal of the Gay and Lesbian Humanist Association, written by George Broadhead, its editor, with a portrait of me on the cover. More than twenty years later, the February 2013 issue of *The Oldie* contained a two-page interview with me by their columnist Melanie McFadyean, together with a good photograph that she took with her mobile phone.

A big boost to my ego was being included in the Bromley Millennium Hall of Fame Exhibition, which opened in Bromley Library early in September 2000, moved to Bromley Museum in October, and back to the Library in November.

In spite of my disagreement with Bertrand Russell more than forty years earlier over his obstinate cancellation of a C100 demo, I was pleased in 2002 to take part in the dedication ceremony of an English Heritage blue plaque in his honour on a block of flats in Bury Place, Bloomsbury, where he rented an apartment as his London home from 1911 to 1916. His son Conrad, who was the first speaker and unveiled the plaque ('Philosopher and Campaigner for Peace'), was followed by three other speakers, then me. I had been asked to represent the secular-humanist-rationalist aspect of the great man's life, his writing and campaigning. Then the local MP, Frank Dobson, was the last speaker. A video-tape was made of the entire occasion.

Michael Foot was there, too, in his wheelchair. He still remembered my name – which he always dragged into his paper, *Tribune*, whenever possible. He was my favourite politician of all time, and he had the most beautiful wife, Jill Craigie. I attended her memorial meeting at Conway Hall, where a lovely eulogy was given by Barbara Castle, shortly before her own death. Cherie Blair was also present, thankfully remaining silent.

The Guardian (Saturday Review) of 7 December 2002 contained a nomination by Michael Holroyd of my newly

The 2002 dedication of the blue plaque to Bertrand Russell.
Resident's chairman Alan Spence, Frank Dobson MP, me, Lady Russell, Lord Tavistock, Earl Conrad Russell (son), and residents Irene Wagner, Russell Webb and Geraldine Rodery.

published book *Freethoughts* as 'one of the best books of the year'. I realise, of course, that such puffs are marks of friendship rather than objective critiques, but that does not make them any less gratifying.

The highlight of the Conway Hall year in 2004 was the celebration on 23 September of the 75th anniversary of the Hall's opening, and I was honoured to join Polly Toynbee, Richard Dawkins, and the cartoonist Martin Rowson, on the panel of speakers. Two days later, Rowson's comprehensive cartoon of the occasion appeared in the *Times* and, though I was hardly flattered by my caricature, I was both amused and gratified by his description of me as 'The Queen Mum of Secularism'.

In July 2005, during the international conference in Paris on 'Separation of Religion and State', I was honoured with a 'lifetime achievement' award for 'Distinguished Services to Humanism', embodied in an engraved silver plate, presented by the president of the International Humanist & Ethical Union, Roy Brown, who gave me a very flattering build-up. In my acceptance speech (recorded in the *Ethical Record* of July/August 2005), I named as my first acknowledgment the 'good nuns' who indoctrinated me with such poppycock that, once I realised I had been conned, I felt impelled to spend the rest of my life decrying it and warning others against it.

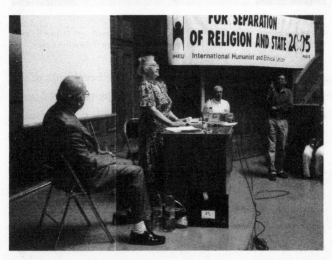

My response to the IHEU award, the Sorbonne, 2005.

While that was taking place in the Sorbonne, Paris, in the early morning of Thursday, 7th July, a spate of suicidal mass-murder and mayhem was being committed in London by Muslim fanatics – presumably riding on the religious superstition of an after-life. Among the 52 fatalities (commemorated by 52 pillars in Hyde Park) was Giles Hart, whose talks at Conway Hall I had attended.

My 90th birthday (2nd June 2013) gave me a multiple ego-trip. On the previous day, a family party, organised by my sister Janet and one of my many nephews, Martin, was held in the extension of the Old Dulwich Woodhouse and was attended by forty family members, who came from near and far – one from as far afield as Connecticut. My brother John and nephew Anthony made speeches (more amusing than accurate), and I responded. Another nephew, Bernie, made a video record of the whole event, and a week later posted it as a 25-minute film on the internet.

The next day (my actual birthday, a Sunday), I was not only given the use of the main hall of Conway Hall for another party, but the Ethical Society also paid for the buffet (including whole salmon and summer punch), which was manned by friends from the Shaw Society. Taking along all the birthday cards I had received, I stood them up along the edge of the stage – and they reached from one end of it to the other! Pasted along one wall were 25 old photographs of me, mostly with other people – including Michael Foot, Harold Blackham and Herman Bondi – which the librarian had unearthed, captioned and enlarged. Silk flowers that came from Bernie graced each table, and the caretaker hung

My brother John

My 90th birthday party, Conway Hall

long strands of glittering letter 'B's down from the gallery. I was also inundated with generous presents.

Deeming the party to be, in effect, my memorial meeting, I had invited ten representatives of various causes and organisations with which I had been involved over the years to come and make speeches. Having attended many memorial meetings as well as more than a thousand funerals, I had often thought what a shame it was that the person eulogised could not hear what was said in their honour. So I, a living corpse as it were, was uniquely privileged to be able to hear (as far as my impaired hearing allowed) the speeches about me, and to read most of them later. The 'keynote' speech – flattering as well as amusing – was made by Michael Holroyd, and the MC was the ever witty Terry Mullins. A friend counted the number of guests, and said it came to 156.

With Janet at the party

The editor of the local paper, the *Camden New Journal*, unexpectedly turned up with a photographer, and half a page of their next issue was devoted to me, with photographs, while a separate piece on another page featured a photograph of Michael Holroyd with me. The party was also covered fully in the July *Ethical Record*, featuring extracts from the eleven speeches (including my response). That was then off-printed as a pamphlet with colour photographs, and there was a shorter version in the Summer/Autumn issue of *The Shavian*.

With Sir Michael Holroyd, 2013

ADJOURNMENT

I had a bit of a health scare in the summer of 2002 and was referred to Guy's Hospital with suspected cancer of the uterus. The ultra-scan I had there seemed to confirm the suspicion, and I was booked into St Thomas' for an exploratory operation. After the statutory two postponements, I was admitted to the gynae ward, starved, and prepared for a general anaesthetic. Finally, on reaching the operating theatre, I was told by the anaesthetist that in view of my age (then 79) she had decided it would be better for me to have a local anaesthetic. The word 'epidural' was not mentioned, but that is what she inflicted on me.

Had I been consulted, I could have pointed out that I had had a general anaesthetic all right the previous year for the carpal-tunnel operation on my right hand, but I was given no opportunity to tell them that. In any case, as the procedure would take only a few minutes, I assumed that I was to be numbed in the groin area for a mere ten minutes or so. In the event, 'numb' is not the word – it was total paralysis from the waist down, and was the worst physical experience of my whole life.

While other patients operated on in the morning spent no more than half-an-hour in the intensive care recovery room, I was kept there for more than five hours. At one point I passed out, and when I came round my bed was surrounded by doctors and I was wearing an oxygen mask. Later, the young male nurse in charge of me said 'Your blood-pressure reading dropped to nothing, and I couldn't find a pulse, so I had to sound the alarm.' That was all I was told.

The next morning I decided there was nothing to prevent my going home, so I got dressed and told the nurse in charge of the ward that I was going, but that I would first like to know the result of the exploratory operation. 'Oh, there's nothing wrong with you'. So the whole charade had been for nothing; there was nothing amiss with my old uterus! 'But you can't go just like that', she said. 'You haven't even got any transport.' 'Yes I have', I replied – 'there's a bus outside'. And I left.

I was of course relieved at the negative outcome, but then I was recalled for a minor gynaecological operation in the same department of the hospital. I kept the appointment for the interview – but only to say that nothing would induce me to return there as a patient.

When my sister Betty succumbed to Alzheimer's disease, I volunteered to donate my brain and spinal cord (to take effect after death, of course!) for the ongoing research programme into dementia. I liked to feel I might be of some use to medical science when useless for anything else. I had to go to the Maudsley annually for preliminary tests, which included brain scans – that is, lying in a narrow tunnel for 50 minutes while my brain was scanned, slice by slice, to a noise like a pneumatic drill – but I am pleased to say that the research phase for which that was required has now apparently come to an end. Of the 1,148 human guinea-pigs said to be behind the researchers' identification of the blood proteins linked to brain shrinkage in dementia, I am lucky enough to be seemingly one of the controls.

I have backed out of having a funeral at all – partly

because of the sheer expense of it – partly because of my brain and spinal-cord being ear-marked for medical research (if still required), and partly (I tell people) because no-one would do it as well as I would! As for a memorial meeting, I have already had mine, described above – and enjoyed it.

The main clue to longevity is, I think, to abstain almost teetotally from alcohol, tobacco and other drugs – whether legal, illegal or (perhaps especially) doctor-prescribed on a long-term basis. It is undeniable that whenever a new 'miracle' medicine is marketed, diagnoses suitable for it rapidly multiply. I share Bernard Shaw's view of the reliance by the profession of medicine on ill-health, and relish my recent response to a doctor, who, noting my almost uniquely high cholesterol level, declared 'You really ought to be taking statins'. (I had rejected them on reading the dire warning on the package, 'Can cause memory loss'.) So I asked him: 'Do you mean if I don't take them, I won't live to be old?' He collapsed into silence.

NEAR-DEATH EXPERIENCES

On the 29th November 2015 I was sitting on a bus going up Oxford Street when I lost consciousness. The bus-driver must have called an ambulance for me, as I found myself later in St Thomas' Hospital (not the department I had previously walked out of), where, diagnosed with heart failure and pneumonia, I was kept until 10th December.

I was privileged to be allotted a five-star room, including en-suite sanitation, as well as a large window looking straight across to the Houses of Parliament, with Westminster Bridge on my right and boats ploughing the Thames below. One of my visitors wondered how long it would be before the building is sold to billionaires and turned into a luxury hotel. How much would my free room cost then? (£1000 a night? Probably more.)

However, one of my St Thomas' experiences was disquieting. A female nurse of Middle-Eastern background asked me whether I had ever had any children. Assuming this was just friendly chit-chat, I replied cheerfully in the negative. 'Then why' she asked, 'do you have a uterus?' At first I was simply amused by this, but on thinking about it I realised she was admonishing me for having shirked the primary duty of a woman. (Never mind the population explosion!)

Ten days after being discharged from the hospital, I collapsed again, this time in a local shop – and was taken by ambulance to King's College Hospital, where the diagnosis of heart failure was repeated, together with reduced kidney function – i.e. simply old age. I made quite a good recovery in time for Xmas, and felt really lucky: no care home for me, thank you!

A few weeks later, on 8th March 2016, another of my feline proverbial nine lives got used up, when I was knocked down in the road near home by a reversing motor. I landed on my back with my legs (up to my knees) under the car – but was again lucky: the wheels ran either side of me.

The plastic hair-ornament I was wearing got smashed into smithereens, and may have helped to shield my head from more damage than the one colossal lump that emerged at the back of it. Police, followed by paramedics, took charge of me for two hours, but I firmly refused to let them take me to hospital for a brain scan, partly because I realised that I would be kept in overnight and I was expecting a workman the following morning. (I had to sign a paper saying I refused to go to hospital.)

The lump on my head subsided within twenty-four hours, only leaving me with pain in my lower back, which made walking difficult for a few weeks. I was prevailed upon to sue the driver of the car, as a lesson for him to look in his mirror before reversing, and my case was settled out of court to the tune of £3,000 – of which the lawyers were allowed to keep £750 under the 'No Win No Fee' ordinance.

A friend tells me that in a library he once came across a hefty volume entitled *Who's Who in Hell*. My name was one of those he looked for in the index (why, I wonder?) – and there it was, with quite accurate biographical details.

Paradoxically, also some decades ago, the Catholic priest-author Michael Seed invited me to contribute to a coffee-table book he was compiling, *We'll Meet in Heaven*, with facsimile signatures of celebrity contributors. I could not resist accepting the invitation, and, though my entry was predictably scathing about the purported Heaven and its supreme Lord, I was allocated half a page—directly under Princess Anne's contribution, occupying the other half. So it seems I am destined to experience a bifurcated eternity!

My one remaining objective is to get this memoir on the road before the Grim Reaper overtakes me.

Nonagenarian

CHAPTER TEN
CHAPTER AND VERSE

THE PRIMARY genre of my writing career has been the polemical essay. In the late 1950s, however, when Kingsley Martin was editor of the *New Statesman*, two of the articles for it that he accepted from me were about Bernard Shaw's phonetic alphabet bequest. He said that though Shaw had been a friend of his I made this idea clear to him for the first time. (He also taught me how to compensate when correcting galley-proofs.)

I contributed to Michael Holroyd's *The Genius of Shaw* (Hodder & Stoughton Ltd., 1979) a chapter 'Man of Letters', on Shaw's alphabet bequest, but was really upset when, having corrected the proofs, I discovered that a young woman in the publishers' editorial department had subsequently altered one of my paragraphs (pages 220 to 221), giving it the opposite meaning to the one I intended – as though she knew more about the subject than I did. When I confronted her with this cock-up, she simply smiled. I inserted *erratum* slips into every copy of the book I came across, but have always regretted that I did not insist on the publishers including one in every copy printed, even if this got the perpetrator the sack.

Just for the record, here is my wording: 'English is the most suitable language on which to base a new world alphabet – and not only because English is the world's most widespread language. It is easier to adapt an alphabet from one language to another by eliminating surplus characters than by designing extra ones to fit into the overall scheme, and English, having more phonemes than most languages, would need more letters.'

Summaries of my Conway Hall lectures over the years generally appeared in the *Ethical Record*, while most of my other articles up to 2002 (originally written for the *Freethinker*) are archived in my book *Freethoughts*. I have also written a few essays for *Free Inquiry* (USA), some of them being chosen for republication by their associated book publisher, Prometheus Books. And the American *Encyclopaedia of Unbelief* includes an item by me.

On 22 June 1981, as mentioned in chapter 7, I gave evidence on religious education to the parliamentary Select Committee on Education and Science. This entailed my submitting beforehand a written statement, which was published by HMSO as a *Hansard* supplement. Being unprepared under cross examination to quote statistical data in support of my oral answers, I was told to produce an auxiliary written statement. Again printed by HMSO for circulation with *Hansard*, this was not only circulated to members of the Select Committee but was available for retail as a general public document, thus becoming a permanent historical record.

HUMANISM

In retrospect, though, my most important writing achievement was instigated by Ward Lock Educational Ltd in 1973, when they published the first edition of my booklet *Humanism*, as part of their 'Living Religions' series for teenagers.

As explained in Chapter 8, it was a series of paperback textbooks for local-authority secondary schools, designed to meet the statutory revamping by educationalists of Religious Instruction into Religious Education. No longer was the syllabus to keep to vague Protestant Christianity; it was to be 'objective, fair and balanced', covering a range of mainstream global religions.

To inaugurate this paperback series, Ward Lock commissioned a copiously illustrated but inexpensive booklet for each of the chosen religions, written by a believer in that religion – and I was recommended by the BHA to write one on Humanism.

For the next ten years Ward Lock constantly reprinted extensive print-runs of the series, but (like everything else!) it eventually came to an end. I was apparently the only one of its authors so reluctant to let my booklet sink without trace that I negotiated with Ward Lock to let me arrange to have it republished. Not only did they agree to this; they actually made a present to me of what they called 'the film of the book', and in 1984 the NSS brought out a second edition.

The next publisher for *Humanism* was the BHA, in 1998, but they made rather a mess of it (and managed to lose all my original illustrations). However, they did introduce an important enhancement – a spine – which turned the erst-while stapled booklet into a proper book. A fourth publisher was the South Place Ethical Society (now Conway Hall Ethical Society), which, from 2005 to 2014, published the updated fourth, fifth and sixth editions.

With computerised assistance from Norman Bacrac, I updated and expanded the book again for a so-called reprint, followed by a seventh edition, then a final revised version of that. My purpose was mainly that the best possible version should outlive me – thus affording me some measure of immortality.

My other old book, the 239-page *Freethoughts*, comprising articles I had written over the years for *The Freethinker,* having been Kindle-ised for Amazon by the atheistic publishers G W Foote Ltd, I handed the internet copyright in *Humanism* over to them, and in 2017 they put that too on Amazon Kindle. (It could then be read 'on-line' or downloaded for £4.99 – as opposed to £6.50 to purchase the actual book – and would presumably seduce a wider readership.)

Meanwhile, I have managed to resist the social pressure to own a computer – thus avoiding all the cyber viruses, hacks and fraud associated with the internet, not to mention saving the time required to write this memoir.

THESES

Early in 1985 I wrote an article for *The Freethinker* on embryo research, and it was reprinted as an illustrated pamphlet, *Eggs Are Not People,* a copy of which the National Secular Society sent to every member of Parliament ahead of the vote on Enoch Powell's Unborn Children (Protection) Bill – which was then, unexpectedly, defeated.

That same year I wrote a little play, *Atheism on a Soapbox*, humorously based on my experience on the weekly City open-air atheist platform (no longer existent) that I took over when Len Ebury died. At first I marketed the play as a pamphlet, then a group of amateur actors recorded it for reproduction on CDs, which continued to be sold until that form of recording was superseded.

Also in 1985, shortly before the end of my stint as chairman of the Voluntary Euthanasia Society, I compiled the 303-page symposium *Voluntary Euthanasia: Experts debate the right to die*. One of the chapters – a hard hitting rejoinder to an absolutist Catholic Juggernaut – I contributed myself, and I coaxed a compassionate chapter out of Christian Barnard, the South African surgeon famous for the first viable human heart transplant. The book was published successfully by Peter Owen in 1986, and I donated my royalties to the VES – but might have been less generous had I foreseen that the society would, some twenty years later, weaken its aims and change its name euphemistically to Dignity in Dying.

In 1988 Penguin Books published an educational booklet entitled *Whose Side Are You On?*, for use in secondary schools as a basis for discussion. At each opening there were two articles, on opposite pages, representing opposite sides of the same ethical theme, and I think I was the only author asked to cover two different subjects. One of them, unsurprisingly, was Humanism; the other was infant euthanasia.

There was no shortage of named writers willing to stand

up for *voluntary* euthanasia, but it seemed I was the only one willing to tackle rationally the question of seriously defective neonates. Even the writers in favour of voluntary euthanasia were mostly opposed to sanctioning euthanasia for the newborn, since it obviously could not be voluntary. But it should be termed non-voluntary rather than involuntary – which more properly refers to murder, such as the Nazis carried out.

Keeping these unfortunates alive until they are able (if ever) to choose for themselves whether to die without further delay is to condemn them meanwhile to an intolerable life, and is, I argued, no less a decision on their behalf than granting them an immediate painless death. Realistically, non-voluntary euthanasia for the new-born is like a very late abortion – for at birth, before bonding, an infant is no more than a potential person.

For years I received hate mail from schoolchildren, calling me a baby killer.

LATER JOURNALISM

News that the late Mohammed Emwazi (nicknamed Jihadi John) was 'radicalised' at the University of Westminster prompted me to write an article, 'Educated for Murder', describing my personal experience of this malpractice at places of tertiary education during the 25 years I was president of the National Secular Society. The British journal *New Humanist* rejected the article, but (through Nigel Sinnott) it was published in May 2016 in the *Australian Humanist*.

Already well into my nineties, I then took the liberty of venturing into philosophical physics – first with an essay entitled 'Existence', published in *Philosophy Now* in 2015, then as a sort of sequel to it, a more speculative article, 'The Eternity of Time'. I failed to get the latter published in Britain, but was delighted when it was accepted by the distinguished American journal *Free Inquiry*. It finally appeared in their August 2017 issue, with an excellent editorial introduction. Two of my earlier articles which originally appeared in *Free Inquiry* had been selected for inclusion in its book compilations: 'Should we Respect Religion?' (from 2006) in *The Harm Done by Religion* and 'Why I am not an Agnostic' (from 2013) in *The Faith I Left Behind*.

In that 2017 article I dare to argue, in opposition to most present-day physicists (including Stephen Hawking), that while it is clearly established in physics that cosmic space-time originated with the Big-Bang less than 14 billion years ago, that is not to say that time itself, devoid of space, had no previous existence. Indeed, to my mind it must surely be eternal.

HJB

I honoured H J Blackham with two publications that were really labours of love. One, a mere booklet, I named *Blackham's Best*. It was an anthology of short quotations that I had culled from his writings. Harold said a more appropriate title would be 'Blackham Butchered' – though I think he actually liked it. The booklet ran to three editions, the last two having a lovely photograph of Harold on the cover, produced by William Wynne-Willson.

The other Blackham book I had a hand in was my edited version of a monumental work of his old age, called

'*The Upshot of History*'. Its length – that of a Victorian three-volume novel – meant he was unable to find a publisher for it. Until, that is, I persuaded the American humanist philosopher Paul Kurtz, who was an admirer of his, to take it on for Prometheus Books – on condition that I would reduce the text by two thirds. Needless to say, it took me months.

As for the original title, the word 'upshot' suggested that history had come to an end, which was contrary to H J's intention. Furthermore, I was told by the publishers that the word was virtually unknown in America. So I retitled the book *The Future of our Past*, asking Harold if that was all right. He accepted it, though really too old by then to make an authentic decision. Anyway, the book, published under my title, pleased him. Me too. And he made me his literary executor.

With H J Blackham at his hundredth birthday party

RHYME AND REASON

I obviously inherit my love of quirky wordage from my father, who loved to recite rhyming Edwardian monologues, several of which he knew by heart. He also made up limericks about the family and used to enter the slogan competitions that were popular in his day – such as 'Bullets' in *John Bull*.

Literary competitions being a particular hobby of mine, I have written innumerable short items over the years as competition entries. Beginning in the 1930s, when I used to regularly enter the monthly writing competition in *The Catholic Children's Realm*, I have had many competition successes – mostly but not exclusively in verse – in the *New Statesman*, *Spectator*, *Literary Review*, *Oldie*, and other journals.

Sadly, my erstwhile favourite competition muse, the *New Statesman* – for which, in the 1950s and '60s, I used to take a turn at setting and judging the weekly competition – suddenly decided in 2016 to abolish both its literary competition and its more recent photographic caption contest. The space they occupied was allegedly required for important articles – although many of those published would actually be improved by some judicious cutting. Anyway, both competitions together took up just one (inexpensive) page, so the real reason can only be editorial antipathy.

One of my *New Statesman* prizes was for a summary of a famous historical speech. The speech I chose was the Sermon on the Mount – my version adding a touch of cynicism to 'Love your enemies'.

The best of my verses is probably 'Living Relay' – and it

is almost certainly the only poem ever written with the aid of a calculator. (It was awarded a prize in the *Literary Review*.)

LIVING RELAY

In this, the only world we know,
as people come so people go,

Not one alive was living when
Charles Dickens held a restless pen –
yet as a child I met a man
who'd known him. Such a living span
takes only two. If six we link,
then Shakespeare dips a quill in ink.
If twenty-one? Mohammed gives
to scribes a screed, through which he lives.
Choose thirty ... join the multitude
for which Christ Jesus conjures food;
on thirty-six, with Plato feast;
two more for sages of the East.
Count forty-three ... hear Homer tell
the Trojan tale he'd heard as well.
One hundred, say ... salute the day
when writing starts, with signs on clay.
Two thousand ... and we're face to face
with founders of the human race.

Yes, each has been and each has gone;
yet each a torch has handed on.

Since the famous Coleridge title *The Rime of the Ancient Mariner* suggests a single 'rime', I re-wrote the poem accordingly in 1996 for the *Spectator*.

THE MARINER'S RIME

An albatross doth tireless fly
Above our ship; the breeze is high –
But when the bird with a bow shoot I,
The ship, becalm'd, doth lifeless lie;
Then round my neck my shipmates tie
The bird's stiff corpse. For days awry,
A copper sky hangs hot and dry.
Of thirst now ev'ry man will die –
Save one, who's curs'd by each dying eye.
Hell-bound for aye, a prayer I cry.
At once the wind and rain reply:
The ship doth sigh and homeward hie.
E'er since, I thrust on passers-by
My tale of horror: thus I try
My hapless soul to purify.

And another plagiary verse:

WORDSWORTH VARIATION

With Conti-tours I strolled along
In glaring, Grecian, April heat,
When all at once I saw a throng,
A squirm of tadpoles at my feet.

Their puddle shrinking fast away
Could hardly last another day.

A few weeks since, in weather cool
And damp, some frogs their spawn had shot
Into the seeming perfect pool;
But soon the sun shone daily hot
And drained the water, parching gills ....
How far from Wordsworth's daffodils!

But like his number, roundly guessed,
Two thousand saw I at a glance,
The outer wrigglers inward pressed,
Jerking their tails in frantic dance.
No creature there would ever know
How tadpoles into frogs may grow.

Now, oft when on my couch I lie
In vacant or in pensive mood,
They flash upon that inward eye
Which is the bane of solitude;
And then black anguish fills my heart:
How life bids fair, but to depart.

My attempt at explaining in rhyme the philosophical free-will/determinism enigma appears in the latest editions of *Humanism*, but its brevity excuses its repetition here.

FREEWILL?

Opposing Hume's deterministic view,
Freewill for humankind did Kant infer
To justify God's ire when people err.
Which view is true? Has Hume or Kant won through?
While you can choose to do what you prefer,
You cannot choose what you prefer to do:
Your innate feelings make a constant spur
Unless life's imprint moulds a different you.

BIOGRAPHICAL POEMS

One of my later poems, which won a prize in the *Spectator*
in November 2010, astonished people who knew me, as it
was actually a biographical eulogy of a pope. But he was
the only genuine reforming pope ever – a resolute reformer
of the Catholic Church. Here is my poem about Pope John
XXIII (1958 – 63).

POPE JOHN

Because he'd make a pliant, stop-gap pope,
They voted for Roncalli – whereupon,
When asked his choice of papal name, he plumped
Unpliantly for the *non-grata* John.

In 1415, John the twenty-third –
Of all the many brutal popes the worst –
Was forcibly deposed; since when, his name
(The topmost hitherto for popes) was cursed.

In 1958, Roncalli seized it,
Repeating the same number, twenty-three –
Thus vindicating every decent John
By breaking one bad apple off the tree.

He quickly called the modernising Council;
Befriended 'heretics' and commies too;
He took some steps to sanction birth control
But sadly died too soon to see it through.

The immense public reaction to the tragic death of Princess Diana prompted me to compose the following verse, published in the *Literary Review* of November 1997.

THE STRENGTH OF FRAILTY

A graceful feminine physique
outlives the brawn of men,
just as the mightiest weapon is
defeated by the pen.

Such fragile things as fishes' fins
and sea-fern fronds withstand
the force of flowing waters
that crush great rocks to sand.

Uprooting trees and chimney-pots,
destructive gusts of air
an insect's wing, translucent, or
a waving grass-blade spare.

The gossamer, so delicate,
stays sparkling in the rain,
which, causing landslides, topples walls.
The pliant take the strain.

The permanence of plastic blooms
would not express so much
as wind-blown petals left to bless
a dead princess's touch.

In the first chapter of this memoir I mentioned my poem
'Felix', inspired by my demented aunt Edie and her toy cat.

FELIX

'When the boys come home from the front', she said,
I'll choose the one that I shall wed'
Forgetting in her hazy head,
The eighty years her beaux lay dead.

For fifty years she'd lived alone
With none but cats to call her own;
And now she's in that nursing home.
Bereft of everything she'd known.

Her visitors look far too old
To be the people she is told.
Her face is blank, her heart is cold,
For lack of a hero's hand to hold.

Until, although no soldier-boy,
A cuddly new love brings her joy:
Her idle arms find fresh employ
To stroke her furry feline toy.

RELIGION RIDICULED

My illustrated booklet of rhymed jocular invective, *GOOD GOD! – a string of verses to tie up the deity*, for which I found a superlative illustrator, was published by Bachmann & Turner (London) in 1976. At that time blasphemy still featured in British common law, and shortly after publication the book was officially cited as 'probably blasphemous' ('probably' because it had never been tested in court). It would now be considered an innocuous quip. And though the litigious moralist of the day, Mary Whitehouse, did me the honour of denouncing me in her autobiography, I was never prosecuted for blasphemy.

THE FALL

Suppose God planned the perfect plan,
why let what Adam ate
destroy it all, for beast and man,
whilst blaming Eve, his mate?

Suppose the tree tabooed in Eden
had borne no fruit at all,
so nothing sinful could be eaten –
there would have been no Fall.

Suppose that God's blue-printed Earth
were pristinely persistent,
there'd be no death, and hence no birth –
no you nor I existent.

Suppose that Genesis be true:
our global population
would have ever totalled two
had there been no temptation.

Suppose creationists prove wise
in swallowing the Fall –
what sort of God would victimise
all creatures great and small?

An incredibly popular hymn from the 19th-century *Hymns for Little Children* (little children, and other immature people, being bamboozled as always by religion) cries out for sarcastic parody – and I could not resist trying my hand at it.

ALL THINGS

All things grim and horrible,
All creatures doomed to pain,
Since predators and parasites
And dread diseases reign –
Were these things planned by thee, O Lord,
When instituting birth?
If so (good God!) then hast thou cursed
Our native planet, Earth.

The goddites say specific faith
Bestows prospective bliss,
But how could any other world
Undo the wrongs in this?
If thine the power to make life good
Yet heedless let it be,
What cause have human victims to
Apotheosise thee?

LIMERICK

On a lighter note, here is a limerick, for which I resolutely set myself the task of finding rhymes for my neighbouring town of Beckenham. (It won me first prize in a Canadian limerick competition.)

A motor mechanic of Beckenham
Took girl-friends for joy-rides while neckin' 'em.
By driving too fast,
He copped it at last –
Both a maiden and limousine, wreckin' 'em.

ENVOY

I am told that quotations from some of my old writings have been anthologised – thus extending my lifelong career as an author for those publications that do not pay contributors! But that credible kind of afterlife is worth more to me than cheques – though filthy lucre can be laundered.

In the opening weeks of this year (2018), a lump in my

At Charing Cross on my way to meet my publisher, Thornwick Press,
August 2018

left breast began causing me a spasmodic sharp pain, which prompted me to visit 'my' doctor. She referred me to an oncologist, and after a lot of medical procedures, including biopsy, I was diagnosed with 'advanced breast cancer' and urged to agree to a lumpectomy. Innumerable pre-operation procedures followed and the surgery was scheduled for 19th May, following an injection the previous day to colour the lymph nodes purple for ease of targeting. I had not realised the nodes were to be targeted, and throughout the early hours of 17th May I lay awake contemplating the whole thing. My final decision, as rational and irrevocable as the one I made on 5th November 1949, was to back out. The main reason was that the operation, even if successful, would still leave me with arthritic knees, numb fingers, macular degeneration, and all my other old-age maladies. Besides, most of the people I have ever known are dead. If the intermittent pain becomes continuous I will resort to pain-killers, which I have always avoided, and await my natural termination. The medical profession gives far too much priority to prolonging life, irrespective of its quality, especially for oldies.

Each human life is a pinpoint in history, and history can never be re-written in actuality. This haphazard memoir of mine, having reached the present time, comes to an inevitable end – as I must, very soon, myself. I will then be simply non-existent (like God!) – the same as I was a century ago. *Amen*.